The

New Jersey Colony

by Dennis Brindell Fradin

Consultant: Robert B. Burnett
Director of Publications
New Jersey Historical Society
Newark, New Jersey

 CHILDRENS PRESS ®
CHICAGO

Library of Congress Cataloging-in-Publication Data

Fradin, Dennis B.
    The New Jersey Colony / by Dennis B. Fradin.
        p.   cm.
    Includes index.
    Summary: Examines the history of the New Jersey colony from its
beginnings to its achievement of statehood after the Revolutionary War.
Includes profiles of significant individuals such as Lewis Morris, the
Reverend John Witherspoon, and Molly Pitcher.
    ISBN 0-516-00395-X
    1. New Jersey—History—Colonial period, ca. 1600-1775—Juvenile literature.
2. New Jersey—History—Colonial period, ca. 1600-1775—Biography—Juvenile
literature. 3. New Jersey—History—Revolution, 1775-1783—Juvenile
literature. 4. New Jersey—History—Revolution, 1775-1783—Biography—
Juvenile literature. [1. New Jersey—History—Colonial period, ca. 1600-1775.
2. New Jersey—History—Colonial period, ca. 1600-1775—Biography. 3. New
Jersey—History—Revolution, 1775-1783. 4. New Jersey—History—Revolution,
1775-1783—Biography.] I. Title.
F137.F8   1991
974.9'02—dc20   90-22437
                                                                        CIP
                                                                         AC

Table of Contents

The city of Trenton is New Jersey's capital.

Chapter I

Introducing the Garden State

It is reputed of those who have travelled in that country, to be wholesome of air and fruitful of soil, and capable of sea trade....

Description of New Jersey by the Englishman William Penn in the late 1600s

New Jersey is a small state located in the northeastern United States. Bounded by water on three sides, New Jersey is shaped somewhat like a seahorse with its head in the northeast around Jersey City. The Atlantic Ocean splashes against most of eastern New Jersey. To the northeast the Hudson River separates New Jersey from the New York City region in New York State. South of New Jersey is the arm of the Atlantic Ocean called Delaware Bay. Along the state's entire western border the Delaware River separates New Jersey from Delaware and Pennsylvania. The only place where New Jersey is not bounded by water is on its northern border with New York State.

New Jersey's 7,800 square miles make it 46th in size among the 50 states—only Rhode Island (the smallest state), Delaware, Connecticut, and Hawaii are smaller. Yet when it comes to population, only eight states have more people than New Jersey, and no state is more crowded. The United States as a whole averages about 67 people per square mile, while New Jersey has about 1,000 people per square mile. The least crowded state, Alaska, averages about one person per square mile.

The nicknames New Jersey has earned over the years reflect its history. New Jersey was one of the thirteen colonies that England settled or took over along America's east coast between 1607 and 1733. The other 12 colonies were Virginia, Massachusetts, New Hampshire, New York, Connecticut, Maryland, Rhode Island, Delaware, Pennsylvania, North Carolina, South Carolina, and Georgia. In colonial America, nearly everyone farmed, and since its farms and gardens were very lovely, New Jersey was called "the Garden of North America" in colonial times. When the thirteen colonies separated from England, it became known as the *Garden State*.

Americans had to win the Revolutionary War (1775-1783) to break free of England and turn

COLONIAL AMERICA

the thirteen colonies into the thirteen United States of America. New Jersey earned another nickname—the *Cockpit of the Revolution*—because of all the key events that occurred there during the Revolutionary War. Nearly 100 battles and skirmishes were fought in New Jersey, including the important battles of Trenton, Princeton, and Monmouth. Thousands of New Jerseyans fought in George Washington's Continental Army, which spent three winters in New Jersey.

During the 1800s and the 1900s, millions of Americans left their farms and helped transform the United States from a mainly farming to a mainly industrial nation. By 1890, more New Jerseyans lived in cities than in farm areas, and the state was producing a wide variety of goods. Today, more New Jerseyans work at manufacturing and selling products than at any other kind of job, and about 90 percent of New Jersey's people live in cities rather than in small towns. The state's main cities are Newark, Jersey City, Paterson, Elizabeth, Trenton (the capital), and Camden. Products made in New Jersey range from chemicals and packaged foods to television sets and telephones. Due to New Jersey's position as a leading manufacturing state, it has been

A sign on a bridge over the Delaware River in Trenton proclaims: "Trenton Makes . . . The World Takes."

called the *Workshop of the Nation*, which might be its most fitting nickname today. But because many vegetables are still grown in the state—and because it sounds prettier—the *Garden State* is still New Jersey's main nickname.

A remarkable number of "firsts" and "near firsts" have taken place in the Garden State. In 1758 one of the first Indian reservations in North America was created in the New Jersey Colony. A century later, in 1858, the first major dinosaur discovery in North America was made in New Jersey when a Hadrosaurus skeleton was found at Haddonfield. The first professional baseball game was played at Hoboken, New Jersey, in 1864 when one New York team beat another 23-1, and the first college football game was played at New Brunswick, New Jersey, in 1869 when Rutgers beat Princeton 6-4.

Edison's first electric light

New Jersey has also been an important scientific research center for many years. Thomas Edison, the most famous inventor in history, and Albert Einstein, the most famous scientist of modern times, both lived much of their lives in New Jersey. Between the 1870s and the 1890s, Edison (1847–1931) created the record player or phonograph, the electric light, and the first movie

Thomas Edison speaking into his phonograph. This first system recorded sound on a cylinder covered with tinfoil.

Albert Einstein

(which showed a man sneezing) in his laboratories in the Newark, New Jersey, region. Einstein (1879-1955), who discovered a great deal about the nature of the universe, lived for many years in Princeton, New Jersey. Other scientific achievements made in the Garden State include the discovery of the antibiotic medicine streptomycin by Selman Waksman in 1943 and the invention of the transistor in 1947 by physicists John Bardeen, Walter Brattain, and William Shockley. *Tiros I* (launched in 1960), the first satellite to take detailed weather photos, and *Telstar I* (launched in 1962), the first satellite to beam TV shows between the United States and Europe, were also developed in New Jersey.

The *Telstar* communications satellite was launched in 1962.

John Witherspoon

Francis Hopkinson

Grover Cleveland

Woodrow Wilson

The Garden State has produced many famous people besides its scientists and inventors. Reverend John Witherspoon and Francis Hopkinson were two famous New Jerseyans. Both men signed the Declaration of Independence for New Jersey. Witherspoon was also president of New Jersey's Princeton College, and Hopkinson may have designed the first U.S. flag.

In more recent years, two U.S. presidents were closely associated with New Jersey. Grover Cleveland (1837–1908), who served as the 22nd and later the 24th president of the United States, was born in Caldwell, New Jersey. Woodrow Wilson (1856–1924) was born in Virginia but served as president of Princeton University and governor of New Jersey before being elected 28th president of the United States.

11

Several famous authors have also been associated with New Jersey. James Fenimore Cooper (1789-1851), author of *The Last of the Mohicans*, Stephen Crane (1871-1900), author of the Civil War novel *The Red Badge of Courage*, and Joyce Kilmer (1886-1918), a young man who wrote the famous poem "Trees," were native New Jerseyans. Philip Freneau (1752-1832), known as the "Poet of the American Revolution," was born in New York City but lived much of his life in New Jersey.

Many people picture New Jersey as a place of crowded cities and chemical plants, and they are often surprised to learn that New Jersey still has a great deal of natural beauty. The sandy beaches of more than 100 miles of Atlantic coastline lie along New Jersey's eastern shore. Many resort towns

James Fenimore Cooper

Stephen Crane

Philip Freneau

The sandy beaches along New Jersey's Atlantic coastline attract people
from all over the East.

are located along the coast, including Atlantic
City, where the annual Miss America pageant is
held. Farther inland, New Jersey has lakes and
swamps that were left behind by melting glaciers
thousands of years ago. Northwestern New Jersey
is mountainous. Southern New Jersey has the
Pine Barrens, a large swampy and sandy area of
pine trees, wild orchids, and other interesting
plant life. New Jersey's forests, marshlands, and
mountains are still home to a variety of wildlife
including deer, foxes, wild turkeys, and pheasants,
though these animals are less plentiful than they
were when Indians were New Jersey's only people.

Corn was the staple crop of New Jersey's Indians.

Chapter II

The Indians of New Jersey

Hospitality was encouraged, and little girls helped mothers tend the ever-simmering pot, which signified that a Lenni-Lenape family would share whatever food it had with strangers.

From New Jersey: America's Main Road, *by John T. Cunningham*

People have lived in New Jersey for more than 12,000 years. The stone tools and weapons left behind by prehistoric Indians tell us that these early people hunted in the forests, fished in the rivers, and learned to farm.

In more recent centuries, a tribe calling themselves the *Lenni-Lenape* (Original People) were the major Indian group in what is now New Jersey. The Lenni-Lenape probably were descendants of New Jersey's prehistoric Indians. By the late 1500s there were at least 8,000 Lenni-Lenapes in New Jersey and thousands more in Pennsylvania, Delaware, and New York.

Indian women
building family
lodges

Many Lenni-Lenape villages were built close to the Delaware River or its branches. Between 50 and 200 people lived in a typical village. The Lenni-Lenape built their homes, called wigwams, by driving green saplings into the ground to form a dome-shaped framework. Then they placed tree bark, animal skins, and grass mats over the framework to make the walls and ceiling. Smoke from the cooking fire escaped through a hole in the roof. Wooden platforms at the sides of the wigwam served as beds, seats, and storage shelves. The larger wigwams were home to several related families. The smaller ones housed a single family.

Lenni-Lenapes generally married in their teens. A young man showed his love for a young woman by presenting gifts to her family. If the families agreed to the marriage, the couple moved into a wigwam together as husband and wife. The new husband gave his wife an animal bone to show that he would provide meat for the family, and she gave him an ear of corn as a vow that she would grow the crops.

The husband kept his promise by hunting deer, bears, elk, wolves, raccoons, ducks, and geese with bows and arrows. The animals provided the Indians with a lot more than meat. The animal skins were made into blankets, moccasins, and leggings. Teeth and feathers made pretty decorations, while small bones became fishing hooks and needles. The men also made canoes and fished in New Jersey's rivers and streams.

True to her pledge, the Lenni-Lenape wife grew corn, beans, and squash. Like European women more than 3,000 miles away, the wife also did most of the household work such as cooking, making clothes, and raising children.

Like other American Indians, the Lenni-Lenape were very tender and loving toward their children. Parents rarely hit their children, for fear that the Creator would think the young people weren't

This drawing shows a Lenni-Lenape family wearing black-and-white wampum beads made from shells.

wanted and take them back to the spirit world. Children who misbehaved might have cold water thrown on them. This usually shamed them into improving their ways.

Lenni-Lenape children did not go to school, but instead learned through real-life experiences. Boys learned to hunt, fish, and build canoes and wigwams by working with their fathers. Girls learned to farm, cook, and sew by helping their mothers. Grandparents often lived with the family and taught the young people tribal customs and values.

One important idea taught to Lenni-Lenape children was that they must be kind and generous to others, including strangers. The Lenni-Lenape people always had a pot of food ready to share with passing travelers. They were so famous for being kind, peaceful, and fair that they were sometimes asked to settle fights between other tribes.

Although children were taught that nothing was too good for friends or strangers, they were also taught that nothing was too cruel for their enemies. The Lenni-Lenape had no courts of law. Instead, men were expected to take revenge for murders and other serious crimes against their families. If captured, the guilty parties were sometimes tortured and killed, despite the Lenni-Lenapes' dislike for violence.

The elders also taught their tribe's religious beliefs to the children. The Lenni-Lenape worshiped numerous gods and spirits. Above them all was "Our Creator" or the "Great Spirit," who was called *Kee-shay-lum-moo-kawng* in the Lenni-Lenape language. After this supreme god came 11 other important gods: the Earth, the Corn Mother, Elder Brother Sun, Elder Brother Moon, Home, Fire, Water, the Three Grandfathers

19

of the North, East, and West, and Our Grand-mother of the South. During the course of the year, the Lenni-Lenape held various religious ceremonies, including the Corn Dance and the Harvest Festival, to honor their gods. They also believed that every animal, star, brook, and tree possessed a spirit.

When Europeans began arriving in the New Jersey region during the early 1600s, the Lenni-Lenape welcomed them, according to their custom. Some of the colonists would have starved if the Indians hadn't supplied them with food, and some would have been homeless if the Indians hadn't invited them into their wigwams. The Lenni-Lenape were intrigued by the white people's ways, but generally the Europeans looked down on the Indians. They were horrified that the Indians worshiped many gods instead of one God, wore little clothing, and sought personal revenge instead of settling disputes in court.

The white Europeans also scorned the Indians' views about land. The Indians felt that land could not be owned any more than clouds could. They thought of land as something that was used rather than something that was possessed. The Europeans, on the other hand, thought that land could be bought and sold much like any other

Explorers from Europe came to trade with the Indians.

property, in the same way people buy and sell houses or cars today. The white settlers who began arriving in New Jersey in the early 1600s made land deals with the Indians. These deals were written up in the white people's languages, so the Indians were at a disadvantage. They thought that in return for the tools and trinkets they received, they were letting the Europeans live alongside them and share their land. They were crushed to learn that they had given up their right to live on their ancestral homelands. This happened not only in New Jersey but throughout the Americas.

Because of these land deals, the Lenni-Lenape were gradually pushed out of New Jersey. By the close of colonial times in the late 1700s, probably less than 100 Lenni-Lenapes remained in New Jersey. Today, only about 10,000 Indians live in New Jersey, and only a small percentage of them are descendants of the Lenni-Lenape. The main reminders of these peaceful and interesting people in New Jersey are the area's many Indian place-names, including the following:

Cities and Towns	Rivers	Mountains	Lakes
Alloway	Assunpink	Kittatinny	Hopatcong
Hackensack	Hackensack	Musconetcong	Lenape
Hoboken	Lopatcong	Pohatcong	Owassa
Hopatcong	Musconetcong	Ramapo	
Matawan	Passaic	Watchung	
Metuchen	Pohatcong		
Navesink	Rahway		
Parsippany	Ramapo		
Passaic	Raritan		
Rahway	Yanticaw		
Raritan			
Whippany			

In many books, the Lenni-Lenape are known by the name the English gave them—the Delaware Indians. In honor of the English Lord De La Warr, an early governor of Virginia, this name was applied to the Lenni-Lenape and also given to the state of Delaware, the Delaware River, and Delaware Bay. Since the colonists took away their land and destroyed their way of life, it seems proper that we at least honor the tribe's name for themselves—Lenni-Lenape, meaning "Original People."

This painting by Rubens is called *The Morning of October 12, 1492, Aboard the* Santa Maria. Columbus's frightened crewmen are begging him to turn back to Spain. Later that day, land was sighted.

Chapter III

Explorers and First Colonists

It means that the Indians shall know the day when this country is inhabited by another people.

Answer of a Lenni-Lenape chief, when asked the meaning of a comet that appeared in 1680

The banner of Columbus's expedition

EXPLORERS

Vikings (Norwegians and other Scandinavians) may have explored the present-day United States including New Jersey around the year 1000, though this has not been proved. We do know that Europeans, several hundred years later, became very interested in finding a westward sea route to Asia, where they hoped to find gold, spices, and other treasures in such places as India, China, and offshore islands.

Christopher Columbus was the most famous explorer to search for a westward route to Asia. In 1492, Columbus left Spain and sailed west toward Asia, but the Americas blocked his path.

Columbus never reached what is now the United States on that voyage, but instead explored the Bahamas and other islands off Florida. To the end of his life, Columbus apparently thought he had reached Asia, not knowing that he had reached a New World.

Once explorers realized that the Americas blocked the westward route to Asia, they came up with a new idea. Perhaps an arm of the Atlantic Ocean or a river cut all the way through America to Asia. Such a waterway would be a shortcut to Asia. Explorers began probing the North American coast in search of this passage, but as we know today, no such natural waterway exists except across far northern Canada.

Giovanni da Verrazano (1485?–1528?), an Italian sailor who worked for France, was one of the explorers who searched for the fabled waterway across America. In the spring of 1524, Verrazano sailed the *Dauphine* to present-day North Carolina. Turning northward, Verrazano sailed all the way to the Canadian coast beyond Maine. Along the way, he probed bays and rivers in search of a western passage to Asia. While on this futile search, Verrazano became the first known European to explore the coasts of several states, including New Jersey and New York.

Giovanni da Verrazano

Henry Hudson's ship *Half Moon* explored New York Bay.

More is known about the next important explorer in the region, Henry Hudson, who arrived nearly a century later. Hudson was an Englishman hired in early 1609 by the Dutch East India Company, a trading firm in The Netherlands. The Dutch East India Company wanted Hudson to search for a shortcut to Asia through Arctic waters. At that time people mistakenly thought that the North Pole was surrounded by a warm sea and that a ship from Europe could sail on it over the top of the world to Asia.

Henry Hudson

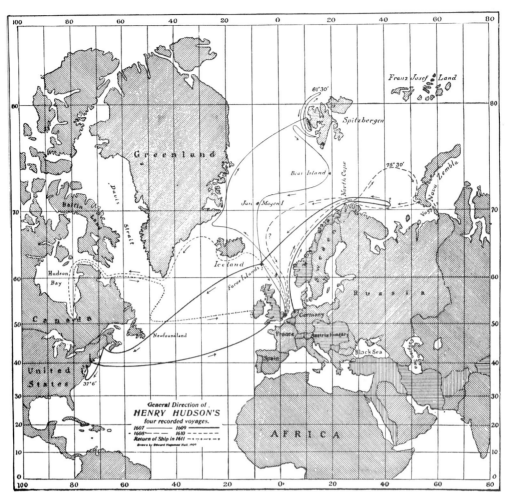

Henry Hudson made four voyages of exploration. In 1611, Hudson was set adrift by mutineers in James Bay, Canada. He was never seen again.

Accompanied by a small crew that included his young son, John, Henry Hudson sailed the *Half Moon* from The Netherlands toward Arctic waters in early spring of 1609. The *Half Moon* was stopped by ice well short of the North Pole. Not wanting his voyage to be a total waste, Hudson then changed course and headed west toward

America. He hoped to find the mythical waterway through America to Asia that Verrazano had searched for 85 years earlier.

Under Hudson's command, the *Half Moon* reached the coast of Newfoundland, Canada, in the summer of 1609. Hudson followed the coast all the way south to North Carolina and then back north again. Along the way, he explored the New Jersey coast and became the first European to explore the waterway that divides what are now northeastern New Jersey and New York, and which now bears his name—the Hudson River.

THE START OF NEW NETHERLAND

As he headed home in late 1609, Henry Hudson was a very disappointed man. Like Verrazano, he had been more interested in finding the western shortcut to Asia than in exploring American lands. Also like Verrazano, he had failed in this quest. However, The Netherlands, one of Europe's most powerful nations at that time, soon claimed a large chunk of American land based on Henry Hudson's 1609 voyage. Called New Netherland, this territory was at first composed of parts of what are now the states of New York, New Jersey, Delaware, and Connecticut. Later, part of Pennsylvania was included.

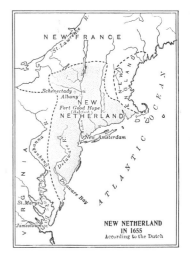

This Dutch map, drawn in 1655, does not show Manhattan as an island.

Flag of the Dutch West India Company

The Dutch settlement of New Amsterdam at the foot of Manhattan Island, as it looked in the mid-17th century

In 1621 wealthy merchants in The Netherlands formed a firm called the Dutch West India Company. The Netherlands' government granted the Dutch West India Company the right to build towns and trade with the Indians in New Netherland. According to the company, no one *but* the Dutch West India Company could trade in the region. At that time, Dutch merchants wanted to trade tools and trinkets to the Indians in return for beaver and other furs that could be made into fancy clothes in Europe.

The Dutch West India Company put most of its effort into building forts and towns in the region that became New York. In 1624 the company

founded Fort Orange (now Albany), the first permanent non-Indian settlement in what is now New York State. In 1625 the company began building a town called New Amsterdam (now New York City) on Manhattan Island. New Amsterdam became the capital and most important town of New Netherland.

Dutch clothing of colonial times

A smaller number of Dutch people moved into New Jersey, Delaware, and Connecticut. By 1624, a New Netherland official named Cornelius Mey had established Fort Nassau on the Delaware River in what is now southwestern New Jersey. However, a Dutch ship that stopped at Fort Nassau a few years later found no signs of life at Fort Nassau, and to this day the fate of the Dutchmen at the fort is unknown. There is a reminder of Cornelius Mey in New Jersey, though. Cape May, the peninsula that pokes out from southern New Jersey into Delaware Bay, was named for Cornelius Mey, with only a slight change of spelling.

The seal of New Amsterdam

In 1630 an official of the Dutch West India Company named Michael Pauw was granted a large tract of land in what is now northeastern New Jersey. Pauw named the settlement he planned to build on this land *Pavonia*, after himself. Although Pauw never left The Nether-

Dutch settlers landed on Staten Island in 1640.

lands, he sent a few settlers to Pavonia (today part of Jersey City). In 1633, two homes—perhaps New Jersey's first non-Indian homes—were built in Pavonia. But because Pavonia was abandoned after a few years, it is not considered New Jersey's first permanent colonial settlement.

During the 1630s and early 1640s a few Dutch farm families moved into the New Jersey portion of New Netherland. They came mainly from New Amsterdam across the Hudson River. Then in

1641 something happened near New Amsterdam that by a chain reaction drove the Dutch settlers out of New Jersey for a time. An Indian killed a Dutchman for no good reason that the colonists could see—but for a good reason according to the Indians' sense of justice. As a child, the Indian had seen his uncle murdered by Dutch workmen. The Indian waited until he grew up to take revenge. Then, unable to find his uncle's murderers, he killed another Dutchman in their place.

The governor of New Netherland, William Kieft, didn't care about the Indians' idea of justice. On the night of February 25, 1643, Kieft sent soldiers to slaughter Indians who were camped on both sides of the Hudson River. The troops who went to the New Jersey side murdered about 80 Indians around Pavonia. They threw Indian babies into the Hudson River and shot the parents as they tried to save their drowning children. Kieft's men also killed about 40 Indians who were camped on what is now the New York side of the Hudson River. When the soldiers returned to the New Amsterdam fort, Governor Kieft rewarded them with medals.

A number of Indian tribes in the region, including some Lenni-Lenape, declared war on the Dutch colonists because of these massacres. The Indians attacked farm families in present-day New York, New Jersey, and Connecticut during the following months. The small group of Dutch colonists in what is now northeastern New Jersey moved across the Hudson River to the safety of New Amsterdam.

Governor Kieft once again sent soldiers to take revenge on the Indians. With the help of some Englishmen, the Dutch soldiers slaughtered hundreds of Indians in what is now southeastern New York. After suffering tremendous losses, the Indians finally agreed to a peace treaty with the Dutch in 1645. Because Governor William Kieft turned a bad situation into a terrible one, this conflict between the Indians and the New Netherlanders is called Kieft's Indian War.

Citizens of New Amsterdam smoked the pipe of peace with the Indians after Kieft's Indian War.

Once peace was restored, a handful of Dutch colonists trickled back across the Hudson River into northeastern New Jersey. Over the next few years, Dutch people built a few farms on a 10-mile-long strip of land between what are now Hoboken and Bayonne, New Jersey. The Dutch families stayed mainly within that strip because they wanted to be near the fort at New Amsterdam, across the Hudson River. A few Dutch people also reoccupied Fort Nassau along the Delaware River shore in what is now southwestern New Jersey. Fort Nassau was occupied by the Dutch on and off until 1651.

NEW SWEDEN'S RISE AND FALL

The Dutch wanted to control Delaware Bay and the Delaware River because they feared competition in the fur trade from another powerful European nation, Sweden, which also wanted to possess these waterways. In 1638, Swedish settlers founded their country's first permanent American settlement at what is now Wilmington, Delaware. This settlement was the start of New Sweden, which included parts of Delaware, New Jersey, and Pennsylvania.

The first Swedish settlement in what is now New Jersey was founded in 1643. Called Fort

Elfsborg, it was located in southwestern New Jersey not far from The Netherlands' Fort Nassau. The New Jersey region was always a minor part of New Sweden compared with Pennsylvania and Delaware, however. According to one count, only about 20 Swedish people lived in New Jersey as of 1644, most of them at Fort Elfsborg. There were so many mosquitoes at Fort Elfsborg that the few people who lived there called it *Myggenborg*, meaning "Mosquito Castle." The mosquitoes, plus the presence of Dutch soldiers at Fort Nassau and across the Delaware River in Delaware, prompted the Swedes to abandon Fort Elfsborg by 1651.

New Sweden was a failure, mainly because few Swedish people settled there. In its 17 years of existence, from 1638 to 1655, New Sweden's population never topped 1,000, with only a handful of those people living in New Jersey. Life was so good in Sweden at the time that few Swedes wanted to leave their homeland. And if Sweden hadn't sentenced some of its petty criminals to live in America, New Sweden's population would have been even smaller.

In 1647, Peter Stuyvesant became the governor of New Netherland. Stuyvesant was an excellent governor who made peace with the Indians, built up New Amsterdam, and avoided fights with other

Peter Stuyvesant arrived in New Netherland in 1647.

nations. In late 1654, Stuyvesant received orders from The Netherlands to conquer New Sweden. That was an easy task! Stuyvesant and his 300-man army sailed down the Delaware River in the summer of 1655 and seized all the Swedish-held territory in present-day Delaware, New Jersey, and Pennsylvania without a fight. Fort Elfsborg was abandoned by then, so there was no threat that the Swedes would challenge the Dutch in New Jersey. Thus, after 17 years of little progress, New Sweden was history. The Dutch, who already controlled northeastern New Jersey, now firmly held the Delaware River side in the west as well.

A FEW MORE YEARS OF DUTCH RULE

While Governor Stuyvesant was off conquering New Sweden, the Dutch started another Indian war back home in New Netherland. In September 1655, an Indian girl entered a Dutchman's orchard in New Amsterdam and picked a few peaches. For this, the orchard's owner shot her dead. The Indians then attacked the colonists on both sides of the Hudson River in what are now New Jersey and New York. Dutch farms along the little strip in northeastern New Jersey were destroyed, New Amsterdam was badly damaged, and about 100 colonists were killed in this brief Peach War.

Peter Stuyvesant was much wiser and fairer than Governor Kieft. He knew that the murder of the Indian girl had started the Peach War. Upon his return to New Amsterdam in October 1655, he made peace with the Indians instead of taking revenge on them. By doing so, he secured the release of a number of Dutch people held captive by the Indians.

Stuyvesant felt that the New Netherlanders would be safer in towns, rather than scattered across the countryside, so he ordered people in present-day New Jersey to build settlements. This resulted in the founding of the first permanent non-Indian town in what is now New Jersey—Bergen—in 1660. A fence was built around Bergen to protect it, and soon the town had a church, a court, and a sheriff. Today, Bergen is part of Jersey City.

Despite Stuyvesant's order, the Dutch did little to build up New Jersey or any other part of New Netherland besides New Amsterdam. The Dutch settlers faced the same problem that had toppled New Sweden. Few Dutch people wanted to trade the freedom and opportunities offered in The Netherlands for the dangers and uncertainties of life in America.

By 1663, New Netherland had only about 10,000 colonists. Roughly 7,500 of them lived in or near New Amsterdam, while the other 2,500 inhabited other parts of New York State and parts of Delaware, New Jersey, and Pennsylvania. The New Jersey portion of New Netherland had perhaps 200 colonists as of 1663. The 10,000 New Netherlanders weren't nearly enough to protect the territory from another people who wanted it—the English.

English settlers in New England. The first colonists endured many hardships before they were able to establish farms and build homes.

Chapter IV

The English Take Over: 1664–1702

During that period they [some of the early West Jersey settlers] lived, in the Indian manner, in wigwams of poles covered with bark, or in caves protected with logs in the steep banks of the creeks. Many of them lived in the villages of the Indians. The Indians supplied them all with corn and venison, and without this Indian help, they would have run serious risk of starving, for they were not accustomed to hunting.

From The Quaker Colonies: A Chronicle of the Proprietors of the Delaware, *by Sydney G. Fisher*

England, which was very powerful by the 1600s, claimed the right to colonize all of North America based on a voyage that John Cabot had made to the continent in 1497. The English began their permanent American colonization in 1607 by founding Jamestown, Virginia. Thirteen years later, in 1620, the Pilgrims founded England's second permanent American colony at Plymouth, Massachusetts. By 1663 England controlled

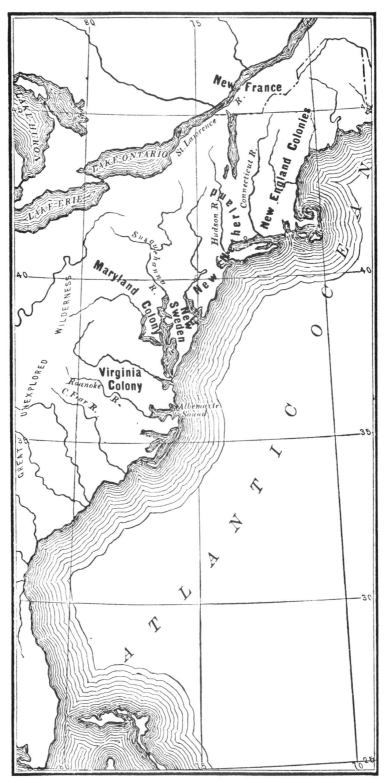

European settlements along the coast of North America in the mid-17th century. The English controlled most of the northern and southern areas.

Maine (which belonged to Massachusetts in colonial times), New Hampshire, Massachusetts, Rhode Island, Connecticut, Maryland, Virginia, and Carolina (which wasn't yet divided into North and South Carolina).

King Charles II

Only three areas along the east coast were not under English control by 1663. One was Florida, which was held firmly by Spain. Another was Georgia, which was uncolonized as yet but would come under English rule 70 years later in 1733. The third region that England didn't yet possess was New Netherland, which by 1663 consisted of parts of what are now New York, New Jersey, Delaware, and Pennsylvania.

In the early 1660s, England's King Charles II studied the map of America's east coast and decided that it was time for New Netherland to come under English rule. King Charles II thought of an easy way to accomplish this goal. He gave New Netherland to his brother, James, the Duke of York. The only "string" attached to the gift was that James had to take the territory away from the Dutch. Since James commanded England's mighty navy, that wouldn't be very difficult.

King James II, formerly Duke of York

James didn't cross the Atlantic Ocean himself. In May 1664, he sent a fleet of warships carrying 300 men under Colonel Richard Nicolls to conquer New Netherland. The ships reached New Amsterdam in August and pointed their big guns at the Dutch capital. Colonel Nicolls demanded that Governor Stuyvesant surrender New Netherland to England.

One reason the name Peter Stuyvesant is still honored today is that he generally tried to avoid bloodshed during his 17 years as New Netherland's governor. He had conquered New Sweden without a fight and made peace with the Indians after the Peach War. But surrendering his colony to England was a sickening idea to the old soldier who had lost a leg many years earlier while serving in the Dutch army. "Peg Leg Pete," or "Stubborn Pete" as he was also nicknamed, wanted to fight. Fortunately, a petition signed by 93 of his people including his own son convinced Governor Stuyvesant that he had to surrender. Stuyvesant signed the papers turning New Netherland over to England on September 8, 1664.

English names were given to the former Dutch colony of New Netherland. The region's largest part was renamed New York, for James, the Duke of York. The town of New Amsterdam became New York City, also in honor of James. Another part of the territory became officially known as Delaware, for the English Lord De La Warr who had served as Virginia's governor years earlier. And the area discussed in this book was named New Jersey—for an interesting reason.

James, the Duke of York, had two friends named Sir George Carteret and Lord John Berkeley who had helped his family. James granted a good-sized chunk of New Netherland to these two men. To honor Carteret, who had been born on England's Isle of Jersey in the English Channel, James named the colony *New Jersey.*

Seal of the Carteret family

Carteret and Berkeley worked out a system by which colonists could obtain land cheaply. All the colonists had to do was pay a yearly rent, known as a *quitrent,* on the land. The quitrents would go to Carteret and Berkeley who were to be called the *proprietors* of New Jersey because they were in charge of the colony. The New Jersey colonists were guaranteed a great deal of self-government and freedom of religion. All this was spelled out in a kind of constitution (set of laws) issued by Berkeley and Carteret.

Berkeley and Carteret sent Philip Carteret (Sir George's cousin) to be New Jersey's first governor. Philip Carteret arrived in New Jersey in August 1665. For his colonial capital, Philip Carteret chose a recently settled area in northeastern New Jersey not far from present-day Newark. He called

Philip Carteret arrives
in New Jersey.

the capital Elizabethtown for Elizabeth Carteret,
Sir George's wife. Many years later, in 1740,
Elizabethtown was shortened to Elizabeth, which
is still the city's name today.

James, the Duke of York, had created a problem
by placing New Jersey under Carteret's and
Berkeley's control. The problem was that he had
also given Richard Nicolls, the conqueror of New
Netherland and the governor of New York, the
right to distribute land in New Jersey. In those
days, it took months to send messages back and

46

forth across the Atlantic Ocean, so Nicolls did not learn that James had given New Jersey to Carteret and Berkeley until after he had passed out a great deal of land. For a while, New Jersey land was granted by two factions—Richard Nicolls and the Carteret-Berkeley team.

As a result, there was much confusion and resentment. Many people who had received lands from Nicolls did not consider Berkeley and Carteret the owners of New Jersey and refused to pay them quitrents. However, the granting of New Jersey land by two factions helped the colony in one important way—it brought more people to the colony.

The Dutch had founded New Jersey's first permanent colonial town, Bergen (now part of Jersey City), in 1660. Thanks to land grants made by Richard Nicolls and Philip Carteret, by 1666 the English had founded six new towns in eastern New Jersey. They were Elizabethtown, Middletown, and Shrewsbury (all founded in 1664), Woodbridge (founded in 1665), and Newark and Piscataway (both founded in 1666).

In addition to obtaining land grants from Nicolls or Carteret, the colonists had to make deals with the Indians to actually gain title to their lands. For example, the colonists purchased

The colonists traded with the Indians for furs.

a huge region around Newark from the Indians for goods that included 100 handfuls of gunpowder, 30 guns, 20 axes, 20 coats, 10 kettles, 10 pairs of pants, 4 blankets, and 4 barrels of beer.

Who were the English people who colonized eastern New Jersey in the 1660s? Many of them had been born in England, but most came from other English colonies, rather than directly from England. Newark, for example, was settled by about 30 families from the New Haven, Connecticut, region; Woodbridge was settled by people from Massachusetts and New Hampshire; and Elizabethtown was settled in part by people from Long Island, New York.

England's American colonies were more successful than New Sweden's or New Netherland's had been, mainly because of the many thousands of people who moved there. America had two major attractions for English people. First, England did not offer religious freedom during the 1600s. Thousands of people who quit or criticized the nation's official religion—the Church of England—lost their jobs and property and in some cases were jailed. Nonetheless, many people continued to oppose the Church of England. One such group, called the Puritans, wanted to "purify" the Church of England by focusing more on Bible teachings and less on rituals and church politics. To escape persecution in England, thousands of Puritans moved to America during the 1600s.

The desire for land was the other main reason that English people moved to America. According to English law, the oldest son inherited nearly all of his father's property. Other family members were often left landless and poor. Many of these people sailed to America where plenty of good, inexpensive land was available.

Most of the English people who moved to New Jersey from other American colonies during the 1660s were Puritans. Since they did not suffer from religious persecution in the other colonies, the Puritans came to New Jersey mainly because the other colonies were starting to fill up while New Jersey still offered vast tracts of land. This same land hunger lured Americans westward over the next 200 years until they had populated the entire country from coast to coast.

At first, many New Jersey settlers lived in huts that they put up quickly to protect themselves from the weather. It was said that some people lived in caves for a short time. As soon as possible, the colonists built houses of wood, brick, or stone. A fireplace provided heat and light. The cooking was done in large pots hung over the fireplace.

Spinning wheels were used to spin wool into yarn.

The early colonists grew corn, wheat, barley, oats, and garden vegetables to feed themselves and their livestock. They also hunted and fished like their Indian neighbors. Instead of using money, the New Jerseyans of the 1660s traded with one another for items they needed. A hunter might trade venison (deer meat) to another family for milk or eggs. One crop that the New Jerseyans grew—flax—was not used for food. The women spun the flax into linen yarn, wove the yarn into cloth, and then used the cloth to make clothes.

Because they wanted their children to be able to read and understand the Bible, the Puritans were a very education-minded group. In 1647 Massachusetts Puritans had sown the seeds for America's public school system by ordering each town of at least 50 families to maintain a school that was partly financed by taxes. Since many of New Jersey's early colonists were Puritans, schools were very important to them, too. Several towns including Newark, Woodbridge, and Piscataway soon built schoolhouses and arranged to obtain schoolteachers.

A colonial school, the boy at right is wearing a "dunce cap" as punishment.

Richard Nicolls gave up the idea of governing New Jersey upon learning that James, the Duke of York, had given the colony to Sir George Carteret and Lord John Berkeley. In 1668, Governor Philip Carteret organized New Jersey's first legislative meeting. Each town was asked to send two representatives to Elizabethtown for the first meeting of the New Jersey General Assembly, as the legislature was called.

The General Assembly, which first met in Elizabethtown in spring of 1668, was at first dominated by the Puritans, who made very strict laws. Thieves and drunkards faced such punishments as whippings, brandings, and sitting in the stocks. Children who were on the streets past curfew (9 P.M.) could be whipped publicly. People who cursed had to pay a fine. One important law passed by the Assembly ordered each town to build an inn for passing travelers.

The General Assembly was soon the scene of many bitter arguments. New Jersey's proprietors, Sir George Carteret and Lord John Berkeley, were supposed to collect quitrents from New Jerseyans. Depending on how the land was valued, these quitrents were only a penny or half a penny per acre. Yet many people refused to pay the quitrents when they first fell due in 1670. They argued that they had obtained their land from Richard Nicolls or the Indians and therefore did not owe the quitrents. This early taxpayers' revolt spread through New Jersey. In 1672, people from five of New Jersey's seven settlements held a political meeting in Elizabethtown. They dumped Philip Carteret as governor and elected James Carteret, Sir George's son, as president in his place. James Carteret was apparently a man of poor character who was willing to oppose his father's interests. The New Jerseyans planned to use James Carteret as a stooge who would do whatever they ordered.

Philip Carteret returned to England in an effort to regain his power. While he was gone, England and The Netherlands went to war, with a strange result. In 1673 a Dutch fleet sailed into New York Harbor and reclaimed New Netherland. For a few

The Dutch recaptured New Amsterdam in 1673. The Dutch commanders gave the English thirty minutes to surrender. When the hourglass ran out, the Dutch opened fire and the English surrendered.

months the Dutch flag flew once more over New York, New Jersey, and Delaware. This made little difference to the people of these colonies, who went on with their lives as though nothing had changed. Then by a peace treaty made in 1674, New York, New Jersey, and Delaware returned to English rule. They remained English colonies for 102 years.

Philip Carteret sailed back to New Jersey a happy man in late 1674. While in England, he had been reinstated as New Jersey's governor. In addition, by the Duke of York's order, any land that had been granted by Richard Nicolls had to be returned to Lord John Berkeley and Sir George

Carteret, and anyone who would not pay quitrents to the two proprietors could have his cattle and other goods seized as payment for the debt.

By 1674, Lord Berkeley was in deep financial trouble, partly because he had built an expensive home in London, England. In the spring of 1674, desperate for money, Berkeley sold his half-interest in New Jersey for the rather small sum of 1,000 English pounds. The buyers, John Fenwick and Edward Byllynge, were English Quakers who planned to bring other Quakers to New Jersey.

The Quakers were a Christian religious group founded by Englishman George Fox in about 1650. They were a peaceful people whose beliefs enraged Church of England officials and many other English people. For one thing, they spoke no differently to a duke than they did to a beggar, because they considered everyone equal before God. Many people also objected to the fact that the Quakers had no ministers, but instead allowed anyone who felt inspired to speak at their religious meetings. Even the Quakers' peacefulness angered many English people. England needed soldiers to fight its many wars with other European nations. The Quakers wouldn't fight in the army because they considered war evil.

George Fox

Quaker woman
preaching in New
Amsterdam

Quakers was a nickname the group was given after George Fox said that people should "tremble" before the Lord. The group called itself the *Religious Society of Friends*. The Quakers, or Friends, attracted tens of thousands of followers in England and in other European nations during the 1600s. The English Quakers were persecuted terribly. Between 1661 and the early 1680s, some 15,000 Quakers were jailed in England, and about 500 of them died because of various types of mistreatment.

In 1676, the two new Quaker proprietors worked out a deal with New Jersey's other proprietor, Sir George Carteret. The three men divided New Jersey into two parts—West Jersey and East Jersey. West Jersey, which comprised about 4,600 square miles, went to John Fenwick and Edward Byllynge and became America's first Quaker colony. East Jersey, which comprised about 3,000 square miles, remained a Puritan stronghold with Sir George Carteret as owner and his cousin Philip as governor. Although East Jersey was smaller in area it contained Newark, Elizabethtown, and the few other towns that had been built in New Jersey as of early 1675.

Map showing the settlements of East Jersey and West Jersey

The West Jersey Quakers settled along the Delaware River. Their first town, Salem (from a Hebrew word meaning "peace") was built in 1675, shortly before the deal dividing New Jersey into two parts was finalized. William Penn, a wealthy and influential Quaker in England, helped organize the settlement of West Jersey. A few years later Penn founded the most important Quaker colony in America, which was named Pennsylvania for his family.

In 1677, two years after the founding of Salem, more than 200 Quakers from England sailed up the Delaware River. At a point about 50 miles north of Salem they founded the settlement that became Burlington, New Jersey. Other West Jersey towns built by the Quakers along the Delaware River included Cooper's Ferry (now Camden), settled in 1681. By that time, about 1,400 Quakers lived in West Jersey—nearly as many people as lived in East Jersey.

Upon arriving in West Jersey, the Quakers endured the same hardships that the East Jerseyans had experienced a few years earlier. Some of them built wigwams as temporary homes, or were invited into the Indians' villages. It was even said that some lived in caves along river-banks for a while. After making deals with the Indians for land, the West Jerseyans built homes and planted crops much as the East Jerseyans had done.

In 1677, the West Jerseyans were given a constitution called the "Concessions and Agreements," thought to have been written by the great Quaker William Penn. The Concessions and Agreements offered West Jerseyans an unusual amount of freedom for early colonial times, and even stated that "we put the power in the people." West Jerseyans were guaranteed freedom of worship, a secret vote in elections, and trial by jury. If an accused person was an Indian, he or she was entitled to a jury made up of six Indians and six colonists. It was rare for the colonists to safeguard the Indians' rights in those days. Historians have called the Concessions and Agreements of 1677 the fairest colonial charter of its time.

Meanwhile, East Jersey Governor Philip Carteret was again enduring hard times. James, the Duke of York, apparently considered New Jersey a kind of plaything he could keep giving away. James had caused trouble earlier by placing New Jersey under the rule of both Richard Nicolls and the Carteret-Berkeley duo. In 1674, James complicated things further by sending his friend Sir Edmund Andros to New York as governor of both New York and New Jersey.

Edmund Andros

For several years, Andros made some mild efforts to turn East Jersey into a province of New York and to tax its people. After Sir George Carteret died in January 1680, Andros became bolder. He told Philip Carteret that he must step down as East Jersey governor. When this warning was ignored, Andros sent men from New York across the Hudson River to Philip Carteret's home in Elizabethtown, New Jersey. Andros's men dragged Philip Carteret out of bed. They punched and kicked the governor, threw him into their

Andros's men dragging Governor Philip Carteret from his bed

canoe, and took him across the Hudson to New York City where they locked the badly injured governor in jail.

Andros then placed Philip Carteret on trial for governing East Jersey illegally. The jury found Philip Carteret not guilty, however. The jurors knew that the Duke of York had given New Jersey to Sir George Carteret and Lord John Berkeley before he placed it under Andros's rule.

Although Philip Carteret returned to Elizabethtown as East Jersey's governor, his last months in office were miserable. He argued with East Jersey legislators, who thought that the governor should

William Penn

Seal of East Jersey

have less power and that they should have more, and he never recovered from the beating inflicted on him by Andros's men. Philip Carteret died at the age of only 44 in 1682, after governing New Jersey and then East Jersey for about 15 years.

When Sir George Carteret's widow put East Jersey up for sale, the Quakers decided to add it to their successful West Jersey colony. Twenty-four men, most of them Quakers, bought East Jersey. These men, who included William Penn, became known as East Jersey's "Twenty-Four Proprietors."

Most of the Twenty-Four Proprietors remained in England, but sold land to people who wanted to move to East Jersey. The people who bought land from them included not only Quakers, but also Scottish Calvinists (Protestants from Scotland who followed John Calvin's teachings) and members of other religions.

In early 1685, England's King Charles II died. His brother James, the Duke of York, then became King James II. The new king wanted to gain a tighter hold on England's colonies in what is now the northeastern United States, because these colonies were starting to act independent in some ways. In 1686 the king appointed his old friend Sir Edmund Andros governor of a new supercolony called the Dominion of New England. Andros went to America that year, and began disbanding the assemblies and other self-governing bodies in the colonies that were to make up the Dominion: Massachusetts, Connecticut, New York, Rhode Island, New Hampshire, and New Jersey.

Andros didn't get around to New Jersey until the summer of 1688. On August 11 of that year he visited Elizabethtown to announce that East Jersey's government was dissolved. One week later he visited Burlington to announce the end of West Jersey's government. The capital of the Dominion of New England—Boston, Massachusetts—briefly served as New Jersey's capital.

New Jerseyans didn't suffer as much as people in other parts of the Dominion of New England, where Andros had imposed taxes and jailed his opponents. For one thing, New Jerseyans had been arguing so much with the proprietors over taxes and other matters that they thought the change might help them. For another, the Dominion came to an end not long after Andros dissolved the East and West Jersey governments.

In late 1688, King James II was overthrown. Once they learned that Andros's friend and protector was gone, people in Boston seized

Andros and packed him off to England. Soon the colonies that made up the Dominion separated and returned to their limited self-government.

New Jerseyans also began arguing once again with the proprietors. They still did not want to pay the quitrents that the proprietors imposed. In 1700–01, this trouble exploded into a near-war. Mobs disrupted courts and beat up officials who represented the proprietors. For example, in March 1701 a mob broke into a Middletown courtroom where East Jersey officials were holding a trial for a pirate named Moses Butterworth. The mob freed Butterworth but jailed some judges and other officials including Andrew Hamilton, who was the governor of both East and West Jersey. That same month a West Jersey mob broke open the jails in Burlington and drove officials who were associated with the proprietors into hiding.

Threats were still coming from the powerful New York Colony also. The seaport town of Perth Amboy had been built in northeastern East Jersey during the early 1680s. Populated by Scottish, English, and French people, Perth Amboy became the East Jersey capital in 1686. New York officials wanted East Jerseyans to use New York City as their port, because they collected duties (customs

Andrew Hamilton

taxes) on products shipped there. Even when East Jerseyans used one of their own towns as a port, New Yorkers demanded that they pay duties to New York City. But during the 1690s New Jerseyans used Perth Amboy and other towns as ports without paying duties to New York City.

In 1698, New York's governor sent 40 soldiers to Perth Amboy to seize a ship that had not paid customs taxes to New York City. Although England's chief justice finally ruled that New Jersey ports didn't have to pay these duties, New Jerseyans feared that the stronger New York Colony would keep trying to dominate them.

What was the solution to the rioting in the Jerseys and the threats from New York? Many New Jerseyans felt that East and West Jersey should no longer be *proprietary colonies* controlled by the owners under grants from England's monarchs. Instead, New Jersey should be a *royal colony* under the monarch's direct control.

Queen Anne

Queen Anne, who became England's monarch in early 1702, agreed with other English officials that the two Jerseys should be united into one royal colony and this was done on April 15, 1702. From that day until the American Colonies broke free of England 74 years later, there was one royal colony of New Jersey.

The city of Philadelphia was founded by William Penn.

Chapter V

The Royal Colony Between 1702 and 1760

Take this Province in the lump, it is the best country I have seen for men of middling fortunes, and for people who have to live by the sweat of their brows.

New Jersey Governor Jonathan Belcher, describing the colony in 1748

Although New Jersey became a royal colony in 1702, it could have had another fate. In 1681, England's King Charles II granted Pennsylvania to William Penn in payment of a debt the king owed the great Quaker. Over the next 20 years, Penn built the city of Philadelphia in Pennsylvania and also sent thousands of people to his colony, both Quakers and non-Quakers.

In 1701, a British official suggested that instead of New Jersey becoming a separate royal colony, East Jersey should be annexed to New York and West Jersey should become part of Pennsylvania. This made sense to some people, since East Jersey did much business with New York City and West Jersey had many ties with Philadelphia. Fortunately for New Jersey, though, it remained a separate colony.

The New Jersey Colony was under New York's thumb in one important way, though. Between 1702 and 1738, the man who governed New York for the English monarch also governed New Jersey. The governor, whose headquarters were in New York City, had most of the power in both colonies. Bills passed by the Assembly didn't become laws if the governor vetoed them. The governor also appointed important officials in New York and New Jersey and headed both colonies' military forces. A special New Jersey Council, composed of 7 to 12 men who were appointed by the king or queen of England, advised him on important issues and served with him as the colony's highest court.

Although New York's governor was in charge of New Jersey, the colony did have its own legislature, called the General Assembly. The government met alternately at Perth Amboy and Burlington, which served as twin capitals of New Jersey. The Assembly could pass laws (even though they weren't official until approved by the governor and his council) and raise money. After

1705, each of New Jersey's seven counties was allowed to elect two representatives to the General Assembly, as were the twin capitals Perth Amboy and Burlington and the town of Salem. As in the other colonies, only rich white male landowners were allowed to vote for the assemblymen.

In the spring of 1702, Queen Anne named a cousin of hers to govern both New York and New Jersey. His name was Edward Hyde, Lord Cornbury, and he was one of the oddest characters of colonial times. When Lord Cornbury arrived in New York shortly after his appointment, people discovered that he liked to dress as a woman! It was said that he tried to make himself look like his cousin, Queen Anne. In 1706, when Lord Cornbury's wife died, he attended her funeral dressed as a woman. But this habit wasn't the colonists' main objection to Governor Cornbury. Even in an age when politicians commonly took bribes, Governor Cornbury was incredibly crooked.

Edward Hyde, Lord Cornbury

At the time Governor Cornbury took office, several New Jersey groups were arguing over power and other matters. The English people argued with the Scottish people, and the Quakers argued with the Church of Englanders, and Governor Cornbury helped whichever side paid him the largest bribe at the time! Once he "fixed" an election for the Scottish people after they bribed him, but then switched to the English side when their payoff was larger. Cornbury also headed a group of crooked officials and friends called the "Cornbury Ring," which made large profits by selling huge tracts of land.

By 1707 most people in both New Jersey and New York were fed up with Lord Cornbury. Lewis Morris, a wealthy New Jersey landowner and lawmaker who had a reputation as a "man of the people," led the fight to remove Cornbury as governor. The New Jersey Assembly began insulting Cornbury and also complained about him in writing to Queen Anne. The queen was heard to say that just because Cornbury was her cousin he didn't have the right to oppress the Americans. In 1708 the queen wrote to Cornbury, saying that perhaps the time had come for him to return to England. This was a polite way of firing him.

The governors of New York and New Jersey who followed Cornbury over the next 30 years were a mixed bunch. Robert Hunter, who governed the two colonies from 1710 to 1719, was one of the best governors in colonial American history. Hunter helped remove dishonest New Jersey

Lewis Morris

lawmakers, lowered legal costs so that more people could benefit from the court system, and promoted freedom of religion. When a tenth New Jersey county was formed in 1714, it was named Hunterdon after him.

Throughout the thirteen colonies, people wanted more freedom, no matter how much they were granted by their English rulers. For example, William Penn thought that Pennsylvanians would thank him for allowing them so much freedom, but instead they badgered him for more freedom, almost from the start. In New Jersey, the people objected to sharing a governor with New York soon after the practice began in 1702. The governor generally spent nearly all his time in New York and favored that colony. By 1728 the New Jersey Assembly was sending letters to King George II asking that their colony have its own governor. Lewis Morris of New Jersey went to England in early 1735 to argue the case, and three years later English officials gave in and granted New Jersey its own royal governor. The first one was Lewis Morris himself, who served from 1738 to 1746.

Unfortunately, Morris seemed to change once he became governor. He fought bitterly with the New Jersey Assembly over the issuing of paper money, the ownership of certain lands, and even his own salary. The Assembly grew so angry at Morris that it refused to pay his salary during his last two years in office. For his part, Morris was so enraged at the assemblymen that in 1745 he called them a bunch of "idiots."

Despite all this political turmoil, New Jersey was enjoying great growth. Between 1700 and 1760 New Jersey's population rose from about 14,000 to about 94,000. The Europeans who moved to New Jersey during those years came from England, Scotland, Ireland, Germany, France, The Netherlands, and Sweden. In fact, many more people came from The Netherlands and Sweden once New Jersey was an English colony than had moved there during the periods of Dutch and Swedish rule. People also migrated to New Jersey from New York, Pennsylvania, and other American colonies.

Besides offering plenty of good, cheap farmland and more religious freedom than many other colonies, New Jersey had another plus. It was sandwiched between two of America's largest cities—New York City and Philadelphia—where New Jerseyans could buy and sell goods. Jonathan Belcher, the governor of New Jersey from 1747 to 1757, once said that, all things considered, New

Jersey was the best of the thirteen colonies for people of "middling fortunes," meaning people of average income.

Nearly every New Jersey family farmed during the mid-1700s, even if they also had other jobs. Wheat was the colony's main crop at that time. In fact, New Jersey, New York, and Pennsylvania were called the "Bread Colonies" because of all the wheat they produced. Corn, rye, oats, and barley were other major food crops, while flax was still grown as a source for cloth. Families also raised cows for milk and beef, chickens for eggs, hogs for pork and bacon, and sheep for wool. New Jersey was a leading sheep-raising colony in the mid-1700s.

Sheep shearing. The wool was cut from the sheep and spun into yarn.

Casper Wistar

By 1738, when New Jersey got its own governor, its people had begun branching out to other professions besides farming. Shipbuilding was vital to such towns as Perth Amboy on the Atlantic coast, and Salem on the Delaware River. Many New Jerseyans also worked as sailors, fishermen, whalers, lawyers, doctors, innkeepers, store-keepers, politicians, ministers, and teachers during the mid-1700s. One new industry that came to New Jersey was glassmaking. In 1739, Casper Wistar, a Philadelphia button-maker, founded the first successful American glassworks in New Jersey's Salem County. Wistarburg, his glassmaking plant, became known as "the cradle of American glass-blowing" because its workers later fanned out to other glass factories in New Jersey, Pennsylvania, and elsewhere. Iron-making was another major New Jersey industry by 1740.

Although Governor Belcher had called New Jersey a great place for people of "middling fortunes," the colony was also home to some very rich and some very poor people. A number of New Jerseyans, especially in the western part of the colony, built large farms called *plantations*. The plantation owners traveled about in horse-drawn coaches, entertained one another at fancy balls, and hired private tutors for their children.

At the other end of the social scale were the black slaves. All thirteen American colonies allowed slavery, and by 1750 about 6,000 of New Jersey's 71,000 people were slaves. Families who had average-sized farms might have a slave or two to help in the fields. A rich plantation owner might have several black slaves.

The slaves were for the most part treated like work animals. They labored long hours at back-breaking jobs for no pay. When slaves bought liquor or broke other rules, they were whipped brutally. Those who ran away were punished severely if captured. Several slaves who were accused of committing very serious crimes were burned to death at the stake.

New Jersey also had thousands of poor white people. Many of them were "indentured servants" —people whose voyage to America had been paid for by richer Americans. In return, the indentured servants had to work a few years for those wealthier people. Although many indentured servants were treated like slaves, they had one big advantage—when their period of servitude ended, they were free to build farms or do whatever else they chose. Slaves, on the other hand, nearly always remained slaves for life.

Some New Jerseyans knew that slavery was evil

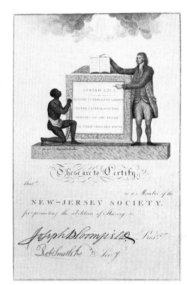

Certificate of the New Jersey Society for Promoting the Abolition of Slavery. In the 1700s, the members of this group petitioned the government to abolish slavery in the state.

and worked to end it. The Quakers led this effort. John Woolman, a Quaker who lived in Mount Holly, New Jersey, not far from Camden, was one of the leading enemies of slavery in the American colonies during the mid-1700s. In 1754, Woolman published an antislavery pamphlet. Thanks partly to Woolman's efforts, New Jersey Quakers came out officially against slavery in 1758. However, slavery wasn't abolished in New Jersey until long after the Revolutionary War.

Some people also tried to help New Jersey's few remaining Indians during the mid-1700s. By 1750, only a few hundred Lenni-Lenape remained in New Jersey. The rest had either moved to places not yet settled by white people or had died of the diseases the colonists brought to the New World. In 1758 the New Jersey Assembly set aside about five square miles of land in Burlington County as one of the first Indian reservations in what is now the United States. In return, the Lenni-Lenape gave up all rights to New Jersey, except the right to hunt and fish in certain places.

Over 100 Lenni-Lenape went to live on this reservation, which Christian missionary Reverend John Brainerd named *Brotherton* in the hope that the spirit of brotherhood would flourish there. Unfortunately, within a few years the

Indians at Brotherton were living in poverty. Around 1801 the few remaining Indians at Brotherton moved to New York.

By the mid-1700s some New Jerseyans had also grown concerned about the lack of a college in their colony. Young New Jersey men (women did not attend college in those days) who sought a higher education had to attend a college in another colony, such as Yale in Connecticut or Harvard in Massachusetts. Around 1740, a period of intense interest in religion called the Great Awakening swept through America. A keen interest in higher education accompanied the Great Awakening, because people wanted more colleges where ministers could be trained.

Jonathan Dickinson

Partly as a result of the Great Awakening, New Jersey's first college was founded in 1746. At first it was called the College of New Jersey and was located in Elizabeth (formerly Elizabethtown). When the College of New Jersey opened its doors in 1747 it had only one professor, Reverend Jonathan Dickinson, who taught six students with the help of a tutor. The college moved to Newark, New Jersey, in 1748, and in 1756 it moved to Princeton, New Jersey, where it has been located ever since and where its name was changed to Princeton University.

LEWIS MORRIS (1671-1746)

Lewis Morris

Besides the thirteen American colonies, British people settled a number of islands in the Caribbean Sea off Florida during the 1600s. The British built large plantations on these islands where they grew sugar and other crops. By the mid-1600s, a British couple named Richard and Sarah Morris were living on the island of Barbados where Richard's brother, Lewis, was a wealthy sugar planter.

During the late 1660s, Richard Morris sailed north to the New York Colony several times to represent his brother on business and to find a new home for the family. In 1670 Richard Morris bought a tract of land almost a mile square in what is now New York City's Bronx section. The following year, just after Richard and Sarah had begun to develop the New York estate, a son was born to them. They named him Lewis Morris after his uncle in Barbados, who then became known as Lewis Morris, Sr.

Tragically, both of little Lewis's parents died when he was less than a year old. When he learned about this, Lewis Morris, Sr., decided to move to New York with his wife. During the many months it took his uncle and aunt to move, the boy was cared for by guardians and a nurse.

Lewis Morris, Sr., who was over 70 years old when he reached New York, decided that his nephew should be a Quaker like himself, and when Lewis reached school age, his uncle hired two Quaker tutors for him. Little Lewis liked to play tricks on his tutors. Once he hid in a hollow tree trunk, and when one of the tutors approached, Lewis said in a scary voice that he was speaking from heaven. The "voice from heaven" then told the tutor to go into the New York wilderness and teach the Indians. Lewis also got in trouble for playing ninepins (a forerunner of bowling) and running races on Sunday, a day set aside for purely religious matters in those times.

Lewis's uncle and aunt complained about his behavior and his friends. The arguing became so bad that when he was about 18, Lewis ran away from home. He went to Jamaica, where he worked for about a year copying important papers by hand. Finally, Lewis's uncle learned where he was and sent a ship to bring him back to New York.

Just a few days after Lewis arrived home in early 1691, his uncle died at about the age of 90. A week later, his aunt died too. His inheritance made 19-year-old Lewis Morris one of the richest people in New York and New Jersey. Among other things, he now owned the huge Morrisania estate in what is now New York City, a huge estate in East Jersey, the first New Jersey ironworks (at the town of Shrewsbury), a sawmill, a share in a ship, and 66 slaves.

The deaths of his uncle and aunt seemed to make Lewis more serious. In November 1691, 20-year-old Lewis Morris married Isabella Graham. They were married for 55 years and had 15 children, including eight girls and three boys who lived to adulthood. While his slaves and assistants worked to make him even wealthier, Lewis Morris devoted his time to books, politics, and his family.

The man who had once played tricks on his tutors amassed 3,000 books—a gigantic library for those days. He taught himself the Hebrew, Greek, Latin, and Arabic languages, and studied law, politics, and history. He also wrote many poems, and near the end of 1715 he co-authored (with Governor Robert Hunter) one of the first plays written and published in the thirteen colonies. Called *Androboros*, it made fun of some political figures, including Governor Cornbury.

Lewis himself entered public service in 1692, when he was made an East Jersey judge and lawmaker. He served as a judge and lawmaker in New Jersey and New York for over half a century. Among his achievements, Morris helped get New Jersey made into a royal colony in 1702, helped New Jersey obtain a separate governor in 1738, and served as the first single royal governor of the state between 1738 and his death in 1746. Unfortunately, Governor Lewis Morris lost the great popularity he had once enjoyed by trying to increase his power and limit the people's voice in government.

One interesting aspect of Lewis Morris as a family man was his supervision of his children's education. Besides making sure that all his children learned to read and write well, he had them debate various issues at the dinner table. He thought that this would teach them to think clearly. He probably also made his family listen to his violin playing, which he himself admitted was awful. Lewis Morris, who died at the age of 74, was the grandfather of two "Founding Fathers" of the United States. One was another Lewis Morris (1726–1798), who signed the Declaration of Independence for New York, and the other was Gouverneur Morris (1752–1816), who wrote much of the final draft of the United States Constitution and signed it for Pennsylvania.

Picture of rural life in the New Jersey Colony entitled *The Road All Along Was Alive With Folks Gwine to Meetin'*.

Chapter VI

Life in New Jersey in the Early 1760s

Hail to the king! whose virtuous heart
Directs his liberal hand,
To stretch over wide extending seas,
And bless a distant land.

> *Praise for King George III, from a poem*
> *written around 1763 by Francis Hopkinson,*
> *later a New Jersey signer of the Declaration*
> *of Independence*

"The Garden of North America" had come a long way in just a few generations by 1760. Less than a century earlier, New Jersey had consisted of a handful of towns along the shores of the Atlantic and the Delaware River. Since that time people had moved inland from both directions, populating much of New Jersey's interior. By the early 1760s, New Jersey had about 60 towns with names, and about 35 others that were called by the name of the local tavern or best-known citizen. Among the towns founded between 1701 and 1760 were Morristown, Millville, Freehold, and

Haddonfield. An unusual aspect of Haddonfield was that it was founded by a young Quaker woman, Elizabeth Haddon, who came to New Jersey from England in 1710 to develop land that her father owned. Haddonfield was also the site of North America's first dinosaur skeleton discovery 148 years later.

Many towns that were tiny settlements in the late 1600s had been built up by the early 1700s. A good example of this was The Falls, a town that Quakers had founded on the Delaware River in 1679. The Falls didn't grow very much until Philadelphia merchant William Trent bought land there and began building up the town starting in 1714. In honor of William Trent, the town's name was later changed to Trent's Town and then to Trenton, which is still the city's name today.

In the 1760s, even New Jersey's largest towns didn't have the busy downtown areas that we associate with cities today. A typical village's "downtown" consisted of a couple of dirt roads that crisscrossed. Near this intersection stood a church, a courthouse, a market where farm goods were exchanged, a tavern, a blacksmith shop, and a general store. Fanning out for several miles were the farms where most of the people lived.

New Jersey's farmers ranged from very wealthy people whose slaves worked their plantations to poor families who lived in shacks and slept on leaves. The typical farm was about 100 acres in size and was self-sufficient.

Most families produced the bulk of their food on their own farms. They made wheatcakes and cornbread from their own wheat and corn, and salads and stews from their garden vegetables. Popular drinks included alcoholic apple cider, peach brandy, tea, and milk.

The typical colonial family also made most of their daily necessities. They saved fireplace ashes to make soap, and animal fat to make candles. Many families made their own clothes, beds, and furniture, and built their own homes. Popping up here and there, though, were general stores that sold such varied goods as mousetraps and earrings, brooms and silverware, pencils and children's books. A farm family traded a portion of their farm products for store goods. The merchants then traded these farm products in Philadelphia and New York City for items to stock their stores.

Most New Jersey children of the 1760s had a hard life compared with American children today.

Shopping in the 17th century

Boy drinking at a well. The bucket was raised by a lever device called a well sweep.

Children generally arose at dawn to help with the farm chores. Although some grammar schools and academies were built in New Jersey between 1750 and 1775, most children had no schooling after the age of eight. Few young people learned more than a little reading, writing, and arithmetic, which was typical in the thirteen colonies.

Although colonial New Jersey was just average among the colonies in educating young children, it was a leader in college education. In 1766 a new college was chartered in New Brunswick, New Jersey. It was called Queen's College at first, but its name was later changed to Rutgers University. As home to both Princeton and Rutgers, New Jersey was the only colony with two colleges. Very few young men could afford college in those days, however.

Rutgers is in New Brunswick

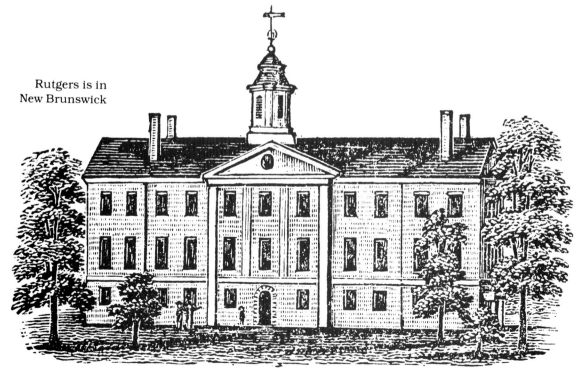

Many important events occurred in New Jersey and the other twelve colonies during the early 1760s. In 1762, William Franklin, son of the famous Benjamin Franklin of Philadelphia, was appointed as New Jersey's royal governor. William Franklin remained governor for about 14 years until New Jersey and the other twelve colonies broke free from England. Also in 1763 the French and Indian War ended. This war, fought over control of North America, had pitted English and American soldiers against French soldiers and their Indian allies. Their victory left the English in command of most of the eastern parts of what are now the United States and Canada.

New Jersey had no newpapers of its own to describe these events. By 1764, New Jersey had not yet established a newspaper. New Jersey's first paper, the *New Jersey Gazette*, wasn't published until late 1777, by which time the thirteen colonies had proclaimed themselves the thirteen United States of America.

One reason New Jersey was so late in having its own newspaper was that fine papers were brought in from nearby Philadelphia and New York City. In taverns, markets, and other gathering places, educated people would read the newspapers aloud, so that those who couldn't read would know about the news, too.

In addition, New Jersey had many travelers during the 1760s who brought news of other areas. Many New Jerseyans traveled between the two towns that alternated as their colonial capital —Perth Amboy and Burlington. They also traveled back and forth between such towns as Trenton, Newark, Salem, Morristown, and Hackensack to visit friends and relatives and to conduct business. And many people passed through New Jersey as they journeyed between New York City and Philadelphia. A network of dirt roads, some following old Indian trails, connected New Jersey's towns and also linked the colony with its neighbors. It is thought that by the 1760s New Jersey had more roads than any of the other twelve colonies. People traveled over these dirt roads by horseback, carriage, or wagon. Many towns required their inhabitants to repair and maintain the roads, and fined people who neglected their roads.

Around 1730, a new vehicle called the "Jersey wagon" was developed. Jersey wagons had huge wheels and canvas tops, and were pulled by teams of horses. Over the next few years a number of stage lines were founded that ran through New

A horse-drawn stage coach and a wagon pulled by an ox team and a mule outside a village tavern

Jersey. One company of the mid-1700s boasted that it could transport a person between New York City and Philadelphia in about 36 hours—not counting stops for food, sleep, and other necessities. Travelers were taken over rivers by ferryboat. Today, a car trip through New Jersey between Philadelphia and New York City takes about two hours.

Because New Jersey was an important transportation hub, the colony had hundreds of taverns. The word "tavern" had a different meaning in 1760 than it has today. In colonial times, a tavern was much like a hotel today. It provided rooms where travelers could sleep, and served food and drinks. In many cases, the tavern was also the place where community meetings were held and where mail was delivered. The taverns were sometimes called "houses" because many of them were located in large private homes.

For those who couldn't read, signs in front of the taverns showed their names in both pictures and words. New Jersey's well-known taverns included the Sign of the Red Lion in New Brunswick, the Rising Sun and the Eagle in Newark, the Sign of the College in Princeton, the Sign of the Green Tree in Trenton, the American House in Haddonfield, the Death of the Fox in Woodbury, the Unicorn in Elizabeth, and the Black Horse in Perth Amboy.

Taverns were never "full" as hotels sometimes are today. People usually slept three to a bed and fully dressed. Those who arrived too late to grab a place in bed—or who didn't want to sleep with someone's elbow in their ear—spent the night by the fireplace in the main hall.

New Jerseyans of the 1760s didn't have the varied entertainment that Americans enjoy today. Generally, the only music they heard was church music and the tunes of fiddlers who played at taverns and parties. A few artists roamed the countryside, charging people fees to paint their portraits. Occasionally, a troupe of traveling actors came to New Jersey to perform plays. The colony's first known professional theater production was a Shakespearean play performed in Perth Amboy by a traveling English company in 1752.

Socializing was the main entertainment of New Jerseyans in the 1760s. The colonists turned as many events as they could into community get-togethers. Families held "barn-raisings" to help each other finish building their houses. Afterward they might have a frolic (party) with singing and dancing. A frolic might also be held at harvesttime or when a family butchered a hog. Also popular was "visiting," which meant that friends or relatives would take turns staying at each other's homes. A family that lived near the sea, for example, might exchange visits with their country cousins in New Jersey's interior.

Now and then the women of an area would gather at someone's home with piles of old clothes

Young people enjoying themselves at a cornhusking bee

and hold "quilting bees." They traded fabrics, then visited as they sewed quilts. In the fall, young people held "cornhusking bees" to liven up the boring job of husking corn. The young people sat in a circle talking and flirting as they husked the corn. Someone who found an ear of red corn might win a prize—perhaps a kiss from a favorite member of the opposite sex. Among New Jersey men, horse racing was popular. New Jersey's state flag and seal still display a horse's head because the colony was so famous for its race horses.

As they did in all the colonies, the richer white males dominated New Jersey politics in the 1760s. The king of England appointed New Jersey's royal governor as well as the twelve-man council that helped him. New Jersey's richer white men elected the General Assembly, which initiated laws and then bargained with the governor and his council to get them approved. The Assembly also had the power to grant or refuse money for projects that the governor favored.

Most New Jerseyans were happy when William Franklin became their new royal governor in February 1763. Besides having a famous father, William Franklin was American-born and therefore might be expected to understand the colonists' viewpoint. Few New Jerseyans of 1763 could have guessed that William Franklin's term as governor would end with his arrest and that he would be New Jersey's last colonial governor.

PATIENCE LOVELL WRIGHT (1725-1786)

Sometime in 1725, a baby girl was born into a Quaker family named Lovell on Long Island, New York. The baby was named Patience, for her mother. When little Patience was about four years old, the family moved to Bordentown, New Jersey, along the Delaware River.

Patience's father mixed some beliefs of his own with his Quaker faith. Because he felt that all God's creatures must be loved, he wouldn't let the family eat meat or fish, or wear clothing made of animal skins. Mr. Lovell always dressed Patience and her eight sisters and one brother in white clothes. White stands for purity and innocence—qualities that Mr. Lovell wanted his 10 children to have.

While still a child, Patience became interested in art. She and some of her sisters made paints out of plant juice and colored clays and then used them to create pictures. Patience also made figurines out of clay or flour dough, and then sewed little clothes for them.

In about 1745, Patience left her home in Bordentown and went to live in Philadelphia. Patience hoped to become an artist, and was drawn to Philadelphia because it was a leading cultural center. This was unusual because, in Patience's time, young women were expected to live out their lives in either their father's or their husband's home. Patience later told a friend that she went to Philadelphia after being "a little disobedient" to her family, meaning that she probably had an argument with them about leaving home.

Patience apparently made clay figures in Philadelphia, but had little success in selling them. It was probably in the Pennsylvania capital that she first wore something besides white clothes, ate meat and fish, and did other things that were forbidden in her strict home. Perhaps it was there also that she became so outspoken and assertive—traits that were rare in colonial women but became Patience's trademarks for the rest of her life.

In the spring of 1748, Patience married a New Jerseyan named Joseph Wright and moved back to Bordentown with him. During the next few years, while Patience Lovell Wright continued to make clay figures, she had more success in producing real-life children! Her fifth and last child was born soon after Joseph Wright died in the spring of 1769.

Patience Lovell Wright now had a problem. Her oldest daughter was married, but she had three other daughters and a son to support. How would she earn money? She didn't want to open a shop or take in boarders as other widows did. Patience spoke to her sister, Rachel, who was also an artist and a widow. The two sisters decided to go into the business of making large wax figures of people. A young lawyer, poet, and musician named Francis Hopkinson probably encouraged Patience in her art career.

Now about 45 years old, Patience Lovell Wright left her youngest child with a relative, then began touring the colonies with her other three unmarried children and her sister Rachel. They went as far south as South Carolina, charging people fees to make wax figures of them. By the time the sisters finished shaping the wax and placing real hair on the heads and clothes on the bodies, their statues looked lifelike. Besides earning money touring, the sisters opened galleries in Philadelphia and New York City where they displayed their wax figures of famous people and Biblical characters. Patience, who became much more famous than her sister, sometimes toured the countryside on her own.

In 1771, Patience decided to seek even greater fame and fortune in London, England. Sailing from New York City in early 1772, she reached the mother country after a stormy two-month crossing. Patience Lovell Wright's work was a huge success in England, where she earned a great deal of money by making wax statues of the rich and famous. Soon after reaching England, she sent for three of her children, but still left her youngest with a relative. The children helped her make costumes for her wax figures.

Patience Lovell Wright became so popular in England that in 1773 she was asked to make wax figures of King George III and Queen Charlotte. Because she thought it was wrong to treat the king and queen like gods, she called them "George and Charlotte." The king began visiting her studio to watch her work and ask how Americans felt about certain issues. But after the start of the Revolutionary War, Patience, in her usual outspoken manner, marched to the palace and told the king that he was wicked for making war on her country. After that, although she was allowed to remain in England during the war, she was no longer one of George III's favorite people! Some historians have claimed that Patience Lovell Wright was an American spy in England during the war. This seems to be an exaggeration, though she did provide American leaders with information about certain British plans.

One amusing story about Patience Lovell Wright occurred on a trip she made to France in 1781–82. One day the French police stopped her to inspect a bundle she was carrying and found what looked like Benjamin Franklin's head. They were ready to arrest Patience for murder! Fortunately, the police finally realized that the head was made of wax.

Patience Lovell Wright never returned to the United States. She died in London, England, on February 25, 1786, at about the age of 61. The only one of her waxworks that survives in its original form is a statue of the English statesman William Pitt (the Earl of Chatham).

Colonists protest a new tax by hanging a Stamp Act official in effigy
(hanging a dummy representing the official).

Chapter VII

The Revolutionary War Begins

Declare yourselves free men.

> *From a letter Patience Lovell Wright wrote to an American patriot on April 6, 1775*

England and its neighbor, France, fought many battles during the 1600s and 1700s for power in Europe. They also fought for power in North America, where France ruled Canada (which it called *New France*), to the north of England's thirteen colonies. Over a 74-year period, England and France fought four colonial wars for dominance in what are now the United States and Canada. Since the French were less land-hungry than the English, most of the Indians who fought in these four wars took France's side. England was helped by thousands of Americans during the four colonial wars, which were:

King William's War (1689–1697)
Queen Anne's War (1702–1713)
King George's War (1744–1748)
The French and Indian War (1754–1763).

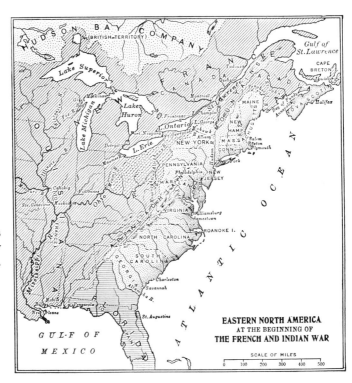

The dotted area represents territory occupied by English colonists.

No major battles were fought within New Jersey during these four wars, but at times New Jersey supplied men and money for the British cause. The first three colonial wars did not settle the issue between England and France. In the final conflict, the French and Indian War, more than 1,000 New Jersey men fought for England in New York and Canada and a number of northwestern New Jerseyans were killed in Indian raids. The New Jersey troops, hundreds of whom were killed, helped England win the French and Indian War. England then took control of Canada and all French territory east of the Mississippi River in the present-day United States except New Orleans.

Partly because of the cost of fighting the war, England had run up an astronomical national debt (the amount of money its government owed) by 1764. How would the mother country pay all its bills? Many English lawmakers argued that the thirteen colonies had gained by the French and Indian War because they no longer had to fear a French takeover. Therefore, they said, the Americans should pay taxes to help solve England's financial crisis. Some English people even felt that the Americans would consider it their patriotic duty to help the mother country pay its bills.

A number of other English lawmakers predicted that the Americans would rebel against these taxes, but they were outvoted by those who favored American taxation. Between 1764 and 1773, Great Britain levied several taxes on the colonists on goods ranging from sugar to tea.

Those lawmakers who had expected the Americans to rebel against taxes were proved right. The general feeling among Americans was that they had already shown great loyalty to England by helping the mother country win the French and Indian War, with little gain for themselves. In addition, many colonists felt that "taxation without representation" was unjust. In other words, since they were allowed no representatives in the British lawmaking body called Parliament, they felt that Parliament had no right to tax them.

One of the first of the new taxes was the Stamp Act of 1765. It required Americans to buy special tax stamps and stick them on legal documents and newspapers. Even a couple wanting to get married had to place a tax stamp on their marriage license. There were demonstrations against the Stamp Act up and down the thirteen colonies.

A Stamp Act official is beaten by the people.

In New Jersey and most of the other colonies, the protests against the Stamp Act were generally peaceful. On September 21, 1765, James Parker of Woodbridge published a newspaper called *The Constitutional Courant* to protest the Stamp Act. (Since it consisted of just one issue it is not considered New Jersey's first newspaper.) Several New Jersey towns including Elizabeth and Woodbridge formed patriotic groups called the "Sons of Liberty." New Jersey's Sons of Liberty pressured the colony's Stamp Act agent into quitting his post.

A tax stamp of 1765

Other colonies also formed Sons of Liberty groups. The Sons of Boston, Massachusetts, were the most violent of these groups. They wrecked a building owned by a Boston Stamp Act official, smashed and burned the home of Massachusetts' chief justice, and beat up some Americans who did business with the British.

When the Stamp Act went into effect on November 1, 1765, nearly all Americans ignored it. In fact, Georgia was the only colony that allowed tax stamps to be sold within its borders, and not many were sold in that southernmost colony. When English lawmakers realized that the Stamp Act wasn't worth the trouble, they repealed it in March 1766. But to show that they still ruled the colonies, English lawmakers declared at the same time that, from then on, Americans had to obey British laws "in all cases whatsoever."

The next year, 1767, the English Parliament passed the Townshend Acts taxing tea, paper, glass, lead, and paints that were brought into the thirteen colonies from other parts of the British Empire. Many Americans responded by refusing to buy British products and by smuggling in illegal goods from such countries as Spain, France, and The Netherlands.

Smuggling was very common along New Jersey's little-populated southeastern shore because the English could not patrol it very effectively. Several British officials and sympathizers who tried to stop this smuggling were beaten up and/or covered with tar and feathers.

Yet even these defiant acts were mild compared with what was taking place in Boston, which was America's most rebellious city. There was so much trouble in Boston that England sent troops into the city in the fall of 1768. Their arrival only made things worse in the Massachusetts capital. Bostonians taunted the British troops, calling them "redcoats" and "bloodybacks" because of their red uniforms, and throwing snowballs and

The Boston Massacre

stones at them. On March 5, 1770, the redcoats shot and killed five Americans and wounded six others during a street fight known as the "Boston Massacre." New Jersey also had to maintain a small British force around this time, but there were no major clashes between the redcoats and the New Jerseyans.

On March 5, 1770—the day of the Boston Massacre—Britain repealed all the Townshend taxes except the one on tea, which was a favorite drink of the colonists. Then in 1773, Parliament passed the Tea Act, which lowered the cost of tea while maintaining the tax on it. The British thought the Americans wouldn't mind the tax on tea because of its overall lower cost. This would prove that the Americans cared more about saving money than about "taxation without representation." Thousands of Americans responded by refusing to buy British tea. Instead, women made tea for their families out of sassafras bark or raspberry leaves and called it "Liberty Tea."

Bostonians dressed as Indians for the Boston Tea Party.

Boston again took the lead in defying the Tea Act. On December 16, 1773, Bostonians disguised as Indians dumped nearly 350 chests of English tea into Boston Harbor. Just as the Boston Massacre had done, this Boston Tea Party brought the Americans a step closer to war with the mother country.

To punish Bostonians for their "tea party," the British Parliament passed what Americans called the Intolerable Acts. For one thing, Boston's port was closed beginning June 1, 1774, causing a food shortage in the city and bringing many businesses to a standstill. Parliament also reduced the control that Massachusetts people had over their government.

People in all the colonies sympathized with Massachusetts. There was a growing feeling that, as the Boston patriot Samuel Adams wrote, "an attack upon the liberties of one Colony is an attack upon the liberties of all." People from a number of colonies sent food overland to Boston so that its people wouldn't starve.

In the summer of 1774, American patriots planned a big meeting to discuss the crisis with Britain. This meeting, the First Continental Congress, was held in Philadelphia, Pennsylvania, between early September and late October of 1774. Of the thirteen colonies, only Georgia failed to send delegates to the First Continental Congress. Five men, including William Livingston, represented New Jersey.

Few of the delegates to the First Continental Congress favored American independence as yet. Most just sought fairer treatment from the mother country. Specifically, they wanted British taxation to end and such laws as the Intolerable Acts to be repealed. Congress drew up letters of complaint and sent them to the king and to other people in England. Congress adjourned on October 26, 1774, but agreed that a Second Continental Congress would be held in the spring of 1775 if British leaders didn't mend their ways.

Britain's lawmakers would not give in, and as a result the Americans became even more defiant. One famous act of defiance took place in New Jersey about two months after the First

The Boston Tea Party inspired other tea-dumping incidents. These colonists hurled tea into New York Harbor.

Continental Congress closed.

In December of 1774, the *Greyhound*, loaded with British tea, sailed up Delaware Bay. Its captain planned to take the tea to Philadelphia, but after learning that patriots there had already stopped British tea from being unloaded, he took it to Greenwich, a town near Delaware Bay in southwestern New Jersey. The captain stored the tea chests in the cellar of a British sympathizer.

New Jersey patriots in nearby towns learned of this, and on December 22, 1774, more than 20 of them dressed up as Indians as the Bostonians had done. The "Indians" broke into the cellar where the tea was being stored, carried the tea chests to the village green, and burned them. This event is known as the Greenwich Tea Burning or the Greenwich Tea Party. The British company that owned the tea wanted to punish the men who had burned it, but because of the anger among New Jerseyans over the Tea Act, no jury would find them guilty. In 1774, patriots in New York City and Maryland also held "tea parties" at which they destroyed British tea.

The First Continental Congress had asked the colonies to prepare their militias (emergency military troops) in case of war with Britain. By spring of 1775 towns in New Jersey and in other colonies were preparing their militias for war. Some Massachusetts militia units were called "minutemen" because they claimed they could get ready to fight in 60 seconds.

A minuteman prepares for war.

Samuel Adams

John Hancock

Early on the morning of April 19, 1775, a British force marched to Lexington, Massachusetts, to arrest the American patriots Samuel Adams and John Hancock. The two men got away, but the redcoats defeated the band of minutemen that faced them on the Lexington village green. This Battle of Lexington, in which eight Americans died and ten were wounded while just one redcoat was wounded, marked the start of the Revolutionary War (1775–1783).

Later that same day, Massachusetts minutemen fought a second battle against the redcoats at nearby Concord, Massachusetts. This time the Americans outnumbered the British. They defeated the redcoats at Concord's North Bridge, then chased them back to Boston, shooting at them along the way. Nearly 300 British troops were killed or wounded in the battle at Concord's North Bridge and the retreat to Boston. The Americans lost about 100 men. This Battle of Concord was the second battle and the first American victory of the Revolutionary War.

Looking back in time, we know that the Lexington and Concord battles began the Revolutionary War, which Americans fought to create the United States. In the spring of 1775, though, few Americans favored independence and many felt that a real war hadn't yet begun. There was a widespread belief that a couple of skirmishes had been fought at Lexington and Concord, and that the two sides would make up, perhaps after a little more fighting.

Governor William Franklin hoped that New Jerseyans would remain loyal to Britain, and he tried to stop them from making more war plans or taking part in the Second Continental Congress. New Jerseyans were divided. Many of them still felt loyal to Britain, but many others strongly opposed the mother country. The opponents of Britain gained the upper hand in New Jersey and formed a new government called the Provincial Congress. After opening in Trenton on May 23, 1775, the Provincial Congress voted to raise soldiers from every New Jersey town for defense against British attack.

Across the Delaware River, meanwhile, the Second Continental Congress had opened in Philadelphia on May 10, 1775. New Jersey sent five men to this meeting of delegates from all thirteen colonies. At first the Second Continental Congress still searched for a peaceful solution to the problems with England. Instead of making peace, however, the British and the Americans fought the tremendous Battle of Bunker Hill near

Boston on June 17, 1775. Although the redcoats took the hill they sought, they lost 1,000 men compared to 400 for the Americans in the fighting. The Battle of Bunker Hill convinced most people that a full-scale war was underway.

Also in June of 1775, the Second Continental Congress created the Continental Army (forerunner of the United States Army) and chose Virginia's George Washington to lead it. During the eight years of the Revolutionary War, all thirteen states sent troops to the Continental Army and also maintained local troops and militias. New Jersey supplied about 11,000 men for the Continental Army and about 7,000 local militiamen and state troops—an average contribution for a state of its size.

General George Washington

Although thousands of New Jerseyans risked and sometimes lost their lives for the American cause, about half of all New Jerseyans were Loyalists—people who supported Britain during the war. Several thousand New Jersey men joined the British forces, and sometimes wound up fighting their own relatives and former friends. At times, New Jersey seemed to be in a state of civil war as the patriots and the Loyalists burned each other's homes and crops. Loyalist raiders kidnapped New Jersey judges and sheriffs who had taken the patriot side. In turn, New Jersey patriots forced thousands of Loyalists to flee to English-held Canada. They also sold the property of hundreds of Loyalists, and even hanged a number of British supporters.

Since 1775, though, the patriots had been in charge of New Jersey's government, the Provincial Congress. By early 1776 New Jersey's patriot leaders had decided that William Franklin must be removed as governor, because he represented the king and stood firmly on the British side. On January 8, 1776, Governor Franklin and his wife Elizabeth were awakened by loud knocking at the front door of their home in Perth Amboy, New Jersey. Armed American patriots had surrounded the house. William Franklin was told that he was no longer New Jersey's governor, but that he could remain at home if he didn't work against the patriot cause. A few months later, Franklin tried to replace New Jersey's Provincial Congress with the old government that had sided more with the British viewpoint. Franklin was arrested in June 1776 and sent to Connecticut as a prisoner of war.

By the spring of 1776 the Second Continental Congress was debating a crucial issue. Should the thirteen colonies leave the British Empire and become a separate nation? Thousands of Americans opposed this, and hoped that the thirteen colonies would return to British rule once the war ended. But with each passing day, more Americans decided that their country was ready to stand on its own.

The Second Continental Congress scheduled a vote on the independence question for July 2, 1776. In late June, Virginia's Thomas Jefferson wrote a paper for Congress explaining why the thirteen colonies wanted to become the thirteen United States of America. This Declaration of Independence would not be needed if the vote on July 2 was against independence. But in case the vote came out *for* independence, Congress wanted to have the Declaration ready.

Most New Jerseyans may still have opposed independence by mid-1776. However, the patriots who controlled New Jersey's government told their delegates to the Continental Congress that they could vote for independence if they thought it was proper. The Second Continental Congress made the historic vote late on July 2, 1776. One after another, every colony but New York chose independence. New York did not vote that day, but made the independence vote unanimous a few days later.

Drafting the Declaration of Independence—Franklin, Jefferson, Adams,
Livingston, and Sherman

The delegates to the Continental Congress thought that July 2, 1776—the day of the independence vote—would be considered the birthday of the United States. However, as most people know, the Fourth of July is honored as the nation's birthday. This came about because the Declaration of Independence was adopted on July 4, 1776. Copies of the Declaration bearing the July 4 date were sent to towns from Maine to Georgia, and so Americans began celebrating the Fourth of July instead of July 2 as their country's birthday.

New Jersey's five delegates to the Second Continental Congress as of summer of 1776 signed the Declaration for the state. The five were Richard Stockton, John Witherspoon, Francis Hopkinson, John Hart, and Abraham Clark. Their signatures can be seen at the bottom of the second column from the right on the famous paper.

The Declaration gave a new name to the thirteen former colonies—"the thirteen united States of America." The Second Continental Congress told the thirteen states to set up new state governments. New Jersey was the third state to adopt a state constitution, behind only New Hampshire and South Carolina. The constitution that New

Jersey adopted on July 2, 1776 (the day the national Congress voted for independence), remained in effect for 68 years—all the way to 1844.

William Livingston

New Jersey lawmakers held the first election for state governor in late August of 1776 at Princeton College's Nassau Hall. On the first ballot there was a tie between Richard Stockton, who had been a member of Princeton's first graduating class in 1748, and William Livingston. The runoff was won by Livingston, who served as the first New Jersey state governor for 14 years until 1790. No one since then has served that many years in a row as New Jersey's governor.

Most people in England considered all this talk about "independence," "state constitutions," and "state governors" a lot of hot air. As the world's strongest nation, England expected to pound the "thirteen united States" back into the thirteen English colonies. During the early years of the Revolutionary War, it appeared that this was exactly what would happen.

WILLIAM FRANKLIN (About 1730?-1813)

Most people know at least a little about the famous Benjamin Franklin of Philadelphia. Among other things, Benjamin Franklin invented the lightning rod and bifocal glasses and popularized such witty sayings as *Early to bed and early to rise, makes a man healthy, wealthy, and wise.* Benjamin Franklin was also a leading American revolutionary and was largely responsible for convincing France to join the American side in early 1778.

Few people know that Benjamin Franklin had a strange personal life. In 1730, Deborah Read became his common-law wife, meaning that they didn't have a marriage ceremony but considered themselves husband and wife. They couldn't have a ceremony because Deborah was still legally married to a man who may have had a second wife in London. Benjamin Franklin had other girlfriends before and after his marriage to Deborah. It is not known whether Deborah or one of Benjamin's girlfriends was William Franklin's mother. The year of William's birth in Philadelphia is also a mystery, with various historians listing the date as 1729, 1730, or 1731.

William didn't get along with Deborah Franklin, but for the first 30 years of his life he was very close to his famous father. Benjamin sent William to Philadelphia's best school and gave him his own horse. William, who was Benjamin's only son (another child died young), went down to the Philadelphia waterfront and gathered stories for his father's newspaper, the *Pennsylvania Gazette.* William designed and built the kite that he and his father flew during a lightning storm in the summer of 1752 in Philadelphia. Fortunately neither of them was killed when a lightning bolt zoomed down the kite string to a key, proving that lightning is electricity. William also climbed up on rooftops to attach his father's lightning rods.

Although Benjamin claimed that it took a miracle to find an honest lawyer, he provided William with the fine legal education that the young man wanted. During the 1750s, when Bejamin was becoming an important lawmaker, he helped his son obtain several posts. For example, after becoming deputy postmaster general for the American Colonies in 1753, Benjamin gave William his old job as postmaster of Philadelphia.

In 1757, Benjamin Franklin went to London to represent Pennsylvania in a tax dispute, and took William along as his secretary. Tall, handsome William Franklin impressed the important people he met during his more than five years in Great Britain. In the summer of 1762, around the time he married Elizabeth Downes, William was appointed royal governor of New Jersey by King George III. William and Elizabeth arrived in New Jersey in February 1763.

William Franklin was in many ways a fine governor. He worked to improve agriculture and transportation in New Jersey, and to help people who were jailed for owing money. When the troubles between England and the thirteen colonies began, Governor Franklin sympathized with the American position. As the king's royal governor, though, he considered it his duty to enforce British laws. In this, William was opposed by his father, who turned fiercely against England and advised William to quit as New Jersey's governor.

In 1775, while Benjamin was visiting Perth Amboy, New Jersey, he and William had a huge fight over politics and remained bitter enemies for life. Many families had such disputes at this time. What made the Franklins unusual was that generally the older people were loyal to England while the younger ones were the rebels.

William Franklin worked as bravely for the Loyalist side as his father did for the American cause. After being placed under "house arrest" in Perth Amboy, William Franklin broke the rules by continuing to work for England. He was then sent under arrest to Connecticut, where he was allowed to live in private homes as long as he didn't help the Loyalists. Once again he broke the rules, and in spring of 1777 he was sent to the Litchfield, Connecticut, town jail where he spent eight months alone in a filthy cell.

Elizabeth Franklin died—people said of a broken heart—while her husband was in jail. William Franklin had lost everything. His wife was dead, his father was now his enemy, and his own son seemed to have turned against him under Benjamin's influence. William sent a touching letter to Connecticut Governor Jonathan Trumbull asking that he be taken outside and shot rather than forced to spend more time in jail. Instead, William Franklin was released in a prisoner exchange in late 1778.

William Franklin spent the last few years of the war in New York City, where he directed raids against the American patriots in New Jersey and Connecticut. In 1782, almost exactly 20 years after he had been appointed New Jersey's governor, William Franklin sailed to England. He remarried and lived there for more than 30 years until his death at about the age of 83.

REVEREND JOHN WITHERSPOON (1723-1794)

John Witherspoon

John Witherspoon was born near Edinburgh, Scotland, into a family of clergymen. His father was a Presbyterian minister, and on his mother's side he was a descendant of John Knox, a famous minister who had helped make Presbyterianism Scotland's official religion back in 1560.

John's mother taught him to read very early, and by the time he was four he was reading parts of the Bible. Thanks to an almost photographic memory, he eventually memorized nearly all of the New Testament. After graduating from the University of Edinburgh with a degree in divinity (religion) in 1743, he was licensed to preach. He worked as a minister in Scotland for the next 25 years.

Not long after he began his career, Reverend Witherspoon had a nerve-shattering experience. In 1707, England, Wales, and Scotland had joined together as the United Kingdom of Great Britain, in which England had the most power. For years, Highland Scots rebelled against English rule. John Witherspoon, who opposed the rebels, was at the Battle of Falkirk in Scotland where the Scottish rebels fought against English troops on January 17, 1746. Witherspoon may have come just to watch the fighting, or perhaps he helped raise troops to oppose the Scots. Although they were later defeated, the Scots won the Battle of Falkirk and captured some prisoners, including Reverend Witherspoon.

The young minister was imprisoned in a castle, perhaps expecting to be hanged. By the time Witherspoon was released a few days later, his nerves were wrecked. He had trouble sleeping after that, and sometimes while preaching he would suddenly panic or even faint. He also developed the habit of yanking at his eyebrows with both hands when he became excited about a subject.

Witherspoons's nervous condition didn't stop him from becoming one of Scotland's leading Presbyterian ministers. People in Ireland, The Netherlands, and the American Colonies heard about him and offered him positions. He finally accepted an offer to become president of Princeton College, and sailed with his wife and their five children to America in the spring of 1768. Reverend John Witherspoon served as the president of Princeton for 26 years.

Colonial colleges were much smaller than colleges are today, and it was customary for their presidents to teach many of the classes. Reverend Witherspoon taught divinity, history, composition, French, and Hebrew. He was one of the first educators to teach American college students by lecturing to them. Until then, most American college students learned by reading books and then giving talks on what they had read. He also taught his students what he called "common sense," which he felt brainy people often lacked. And he was so generous that he paid the tuition of some poorer students out of his own pocket.

Although he arrived in America at the age of 45, John Witherspoon claimed that he had "become an American the moment he landed." He wholeheartedly supported his new country in its fight with England, and was known to say that he would rather be hanged than give up the American cause.

Witherspoon took part in a number of New Jersey conventions and committees during the early 1770s. Then in June 1776 he was elected as a New Jersey delegate to the Second Continental Congress in Philadelphia. He arrived just in time for the debate on whether America should declare itself free of England. On July 2, 1776, Reverend Witherspoon made a famous speech. Probably while pulling his eyebrows, he told the delegates who didn't think America was "ripe" for independence that the country was "not only ripe for the measure [independence], but in danger of rotting for the want of it." That day Congress voted for independence. Witherspoon was the only clergyman to sign the great paper.

John Witherspoon continued to represent New Jersey in the Continental Congress most of the time between summer of 1776 and late 1782. He always wore his minister's clothes in Congress, where he served on over 100 committees and was known for remaining hopeful even when the cause seemed almost hopeless.

After the Revolution was won, Witherspoon took charge of rebuilding Princeton College, which had been damaged in the war. He also served for a time in the New Jersey legislature, and was a member of the New Jersey convention that approved the United States Constitution on December 18, 1787. Besides all this, Reverend Witherspoon did much to organize the Presbyterian church in the young United States. Another interesting note about him was that in 1781 he coined the word "Americanism" to describe an expression or custom peculiar to the United States. Unfortunately, he suffered from blindness and poverty during the last years of his life. Reverend John Witherspoon died at the age of 71 on his farm near Princeton, New Jersey.

FRANCIS HOPKINSON (1737–1791)

Francis Hopkinson

Born in Philadelphia, Pennsylvania, Francis Hopkinson was the son of a well-known judge. At the age of 14, Francis became the first student to enroll at a school that later became the University of Pennsylvania. After graduating in 1757, he studied law with Pennsylvania's attorney-general and passed the test to become a lawyer in 1761.

For a number of years, Francis did little law work. He was far more interested in writing poems, essays, and songs on such subjects as love, science, and the American Indians. A song he wrote in 1759 called "My Days Have Been So Wondrous Free" is considered the first nonreligious music composed in the American Colonies. Francis also played the harpsichord (a pianolike instrument) and invented a new apparatus for plucking the harpsichord strings.

The big question with Francis was: Would he ever be able to earn a living? Sometime around his thirtieth birthday, Francis opened a store in Philadelphia where he sold fabrics and wine, but it didn't do well. In 1768 he married Ann Borden, granddaughter of the man for whom Bordentown, New Jersey, had been named. Francis and Ann Hopkinson lived in Philadelphia for a while but then moved to Bordentown sometime around late 1773. At nearly 40 years of age, Francis became a respected lawyer in Bordentown.

Thanks to his good work as a lawyer, in 1774 Francis was appointed a justice of the peace of Burlington County and also a member of Governor William Franklin's council. But it was after he came out firmly on the side of American independence in early 1776 that Hopkinson did the things that made him famous.

Sometime around early 1776 Hopkinson wrote an essay called "A Prophecy" in which he predicted that the American Colonies would separate from England. In June of that year he was elected as a New Jersey delegate to the Second Continental Congress, and later that summer he signed the Declaration of Independence. One of his most important posts in the national Congress was the chairmanship of the Continental Navy Board between 1776 and 1778.

Francis Hopkinson also lifted American spirits during the war by writing essays, songs, and poems that poked fun at the British. He composed his most famous work, "The Battle of the Kegs," in 1778. This song made fun of the British for being scared of an attempt by the Americans to use torpedoes on the Delaware River. So popular was "The Battle of the Kegs" with American troops that they chanted lines such as the following right on the battlefield:

'Twas early day, as poets say,
*   Just when the sun was rising,*
A soldier stood on a log of wood,
*   And saw a thing surprising.*

As in a maze he stood to gaze,
*   The truth can't be denied, sir,*
He spied a score of kegs or more
*   Come floating down the tide, sir.*

A sailor too in jerkin blue,
*   This strange appearance viewing,*
First damn'd his eyes, in great surprise,
*   Then said, "Some mischief's brewing.*

"These kegs, I'm told, the rebels hold,
*   Pack'd up like pickling herring;*
And they're come down t'attack the town,
*   In this new way of ferrying."*

Great Seal of the
State of New Jersey

Francis Hopkinson may have made another great contribution to his country during the Revolution. On June 14, 1777, the United States passed a law that the nation's flag was to have thirteen stars and thirteen stripes to stand for the thirteen states. Although the story about Betsy Ross of Philadelphia designing this first flag is better known, many historians think that Francis Hopkinson actually designed the flag. Betsy Ross was not known to do other designs, while Hopkinson designed the Great Seal of the state of New Jersey in 1776 and the seal for the University of Pennsylvania in 1782. Besides, Hopkinson later claimed to have designed the flag and there is nothing to make us think that he was lying.

Besides his harpsichord apparatus, Francis Hopkinson created several other inventions. One was a shield that blocked the wind from putting out a candle's flame. He also improved the glass harmonica, a musical instrument consisting of a series of glasses that made musical tones when rubbed with a wet finger.

One of the dearest things about Francis Hopkinson was his open way of expressing love for his friends. In a letter he wrote to his friend Thomas Jefferson in 1790, Francis ended with these two sentences: "I have but few words to spare. If I had but six left, three of them would be spent in saying I love you." Hopkinson had trouble writing by then because he had recently suffered a stroke. About a year later this remarkable man died of a more severe stroke at the age of only 53.

George Washington taking command of the Continental Army

Chapter VIII

Winning the Revolutionary War

*Were our condition ten times worse than it is,
nothing short of the clear independence of this
country would be accepted.*

> *From a letter written in late 1779 by
> Reverend John Witherspoon, who two years
> earlier had lost a son at the Battle of
> Germantown in Pennsylvania*

There were several reasons why the Americans didn't appear to have a ghost of a chance of winning the Revolutionary War. To start with, the British forces were larger and stronger. The largest army General Washington commanded at any one time during the war was a force of about 20,000 men, compared with about 40,000 to 50,000 for the British at top strength. The difference between the two countries at sea was even greater. At its peak, America's Continental Navy had only about 50 ships—compared with 500 ships in the British navy.

Also to the British advantage was the fact that their soldiers and sailors were well-trained and many had fought battles in other parts of the world. The British redcoats obeyed their leaders without question and in return were provided with fine weapons and uniforms. Besides their own troops, the British also hired thousands of professional German soldiers called *Hessians* to fight the Americans.

Hessian troops march off to fight on the British side in the American Revolution

The American troops, on the other hand, were mainly farmers rather than professional soldiers and sailors. Instead of standard uniforms, they wore old farm clothes or uniforms provided by their states. At times, when their clothes wore out, the Americans fought barefoot and in their underwear. As for weapons, many of them used their hunting guns. The American government, still known as the Continental Congress, lacked money to buy ammunition for the troops, and often couldn't even feed the men or pay them. Many of the soldiers had to raid beehives and shoot squirrels to keep from starving.

A militiaman

When it was time to fight, the Americans couldn't be counted on to obey their officers, who in many cases had been their neighbors. Hundreds of American soldiers ran away before and during big battles. And because most American troops signed up for just a few months at a time, George Washington couldn't train his men properly or plan long-term campaigns.

To top things off, few of the American lawmakers at the Continental Congress in Philadelphia knew much about war. A number of them criticized George Washington early in the war for not doing better with his pathetic army!

The American forces had to scrap and scrounge continually just to keep from losing the war. Since its official Navy was tiny, the United States hired about 2,000 private ships, called *privateers*, to attack British vessels. The privateering crews were allowed a certain profit from the British cargo they seized. New Jersey provided the country with hundreds of privateering ships.

Meanwhile, on the land, George Washington tried to avoid the open-field battles that were favored by many European armies, including England's. Instead, Washington made surprise attacks when possible. The Americans had learned this way of fighting from the Indians, and didn't care that the English considered it cowardly.

Partly because New Jersey lay between New York City and Philadelphia—two cities that both sides wanted to control—the state was the scene of nearly 100 Revolutionary War battles. Among them were the very important battles of Trenton (1776), Princeton (1777), and Monmouth (1778).

Late 1776 was a bad time for the Americans. That fall the British drove American forces out of the New York City region. They chased Washington's army across New Jersey all the way to the Delaware River, seizing much of the Garden State

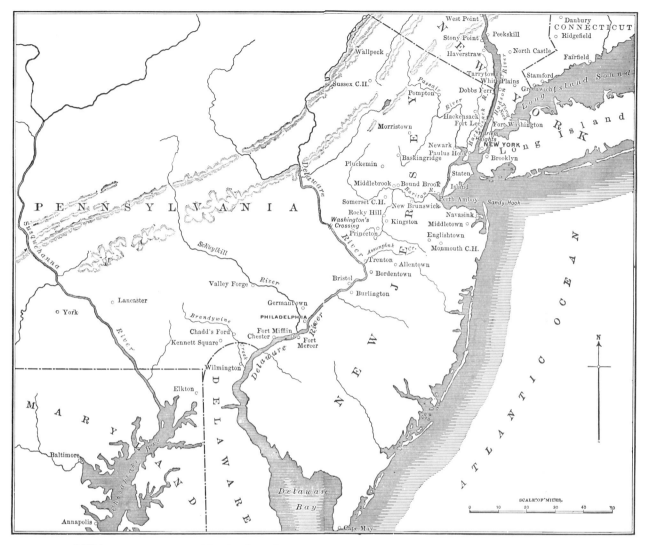

Military operations in New York and New Jersey in 1776 and 1777

while doing so. Washington and his men grabbed every boat they could find along the Delaware River, then crossed the river into Pennsylvania in December 1776. Thinking the American army was just about beaten, the British did not follow Washington's forces into Pennsylvania.

The news that the redcoats had seized New York City and parts of New Jersey was a blow to American hopes. Many Americans feared that the British would destroy the remnants of their army in the spring. George Washington knew that his troops desperately needed a victory to prove that they weren't dead yet.

The British had left Hessian troops in charge of the New Jersey towns they had conquered including New Brunswick, Burlington, Bordentown, and Trenton. About 1,500 Hessians under Colonel Johann Rall guarded Trenton. These German soldiers, and also the British military leaders, thought that the fighting was over for the year. The last thing they expected was that George Washington and his ragtag army would recross the Delaware River and return to New Jersey for more fighting.

Meanwhile, reinforcements from New Jersey and several other states joined Washington's troops on the Pennsylvania side of the Delaware. On December 24, 1776—Christmas Eve—Washington made a bold decision. His men would make a surprise attack on the Hessians in Trenton, New Jersey, on the morning of December 26. Washington knew that the German soldiers would then be sleeping off the effects of their Christmas feast.

Washington crossing the Delaware River before the Battle of Trenton

On Christmas night, fishermen ferried Washington and his 2,400 men across the Delaware River to the New Jersey side. This was the famous "Washington crossing the Delaware" incident that has become part of American folklore. It was what Washington and his troops did when they reached the New Jersey side that made this particular crossing of the river so meaningful.

Washington had hoped to attack the Hessians in Trenton at 5 A.M. on December 26, 1776. Because of ice in the Delaware, the last men didn't reach the New Jersey shore until about 3 A.M.

Nathanael Greene

John Stark

John Sullivan

James Monroe

Alexander Hamilton

After that, they were slowed down again by icy roads on their approximately 10-mile march to Trenton.

Among the 2,400 Americans who advanced toward Trenton on that morning after Christmas of 1776 were several men besides George Washington who left their marks on history. The great generals Nathanael Greene of Rhode Island and John Stark and John Sullivan of New Hampshire were there. So were 18-year-old Lieutenant James Monroe of Virginia and young Alexander Hamilton who had lived in both New Jersey and New York. When George Washington was elected first U.S. president a few years later, Hamilton served as the nation's first secretary of the Treasury. Nearly half a century after the Battle of Trenton, Monroe became the fifth president of the United States.

The Americans didn't reach the outskirts of Trenton until about 8 A.M. First they overcame a few guards, and then they attacked the awakening Hessians, killing or wounding about 100 of them. Among the dead was the Hessian Colonel Rall, who was shot off his horse. About 400 Hessians escaped from Trenton, but about 1,000 others were taken prisoner. Amazingly, only a few

The Hessians surrendering to the Americans after the Battle of Trenton

Americans, including Lieutenant James Monroe, were wounded.

George Washington marched his Hessian prisoners to Pennsylvania, then returned with his men to Trenton on December 30, 1776. There, some new forces joined his army, so that by the beginning of 1777 he had about 5,000 men. In an attempt to crush Washington's smaller army, British General Charles Cornwallis led 8,000 men to Trenton. Late on January 2, 1777, the British and the Americans fought a skirmish at Trenton that is sometimes called the Second Battle of Trenton. Although the Americans held their own in this little-known battle, George Washington knew that in the morning the British would make a much bigger assault.

Early on the morning of January 3, 1777, as Cornwallis and his men slept, Washington and his troops left Trenton by a back road. The Americans wrapped the wheels of their cannons with rags, so that the British wouldn't hear them being moved. Washington headed toward New Brunswick, New Jersey. He hoped to capture British military supplies and war funds in that town, and was prepared to fight any redcoats that he and his men met on the way.

Charles Cornwallis

By sunrise of January 3, 1777, Washington was approaching Princeton, New Jersey, less than halfway to New Brunswick, with 2,400 men when an advance portion of the American force that had gone out to destroy a bridge was suddenly attacked by the British. The Americans lost this first part of the Battle of Princeton, but then George Washington rode up with his main army and led the Americans to victory. About 400 British troops were killed, wounded, or captured at the Battle of Princeton, which ended at

General Mercer was mortally wounded by British bayonets at the
Battle of Princeton.

Princeton College's Nassau Hall, where American
cannon fire forced dozens of redcoats to
surrender. About 50 Americans were killed or
wounded.

The American victories at Trenton and
Princeton didn't just prove that the American
army had some fight left in it. They also inspired

more confidence in George Washington, and convinced the British to give up nearly all of their New Jersey conquests except a region in the northeast around Perth Amboy and New Brunswick.

After the Battle of Princeton, George Washington decided that it was time to go into winter quarters. The army headed about 30 miles north of Princeton to Morristown, New Jersey, which was protected by hills and swamps. The troops suffered from disease, hunger, and cold while spending almost the first six months of 1777 in huts at Morristown.

There were more bad times for the Americans later in 1777. The Americans won the important Battle of Saratoga in New York in the fall of that year, but at about the same time the redcoats drove the Americans out of Philadelphia. Since Philadelphia could no longer be the United States capital, the Continental Congress packed up and moved to Lancaster, Pennsylvania, which became the U.S. capital for a day. After that, York, Pennsylvania, was the national capital for nearly a year.

In late 1777, General Washington led his 11,000 ragged men into Valley Forge, Pennsylvania, where they spent a miserable winter. By spring, more than 3,000 American soldiers had died at Valley Forge. Yet there was great news for the remnants of the army in the spring of 1778. England's old enemy, France, had entered the war on the American side, thanks largely to Benjamin Franklin's efforts. French soldiers, sailors, ships, weapons, and money eventually helped the Americans win the war, but not until they had suffered through more trying times.

The bitter cold winter of 1777–78 at Valley Forge

The coming of the French figured in the important Battle of Monmouth, which took place in New Jersey's Monmouth County near the town of Freehold. Upon learning that a powerful French fleet was approaching, Sir Henry Clinton, commander of the British army in America, abandoned Philadelphia with his more than 15,000 men in mid-June of 1778. Clinton and his men crossed the Delaware River and then marched through the Garden State toward British-held New York City.

George Washington then led approximately 10,000 men out of Valley Forge, Pennsylvania. They crossed the Delaware River into New Jersey and advanced toward Clinton's forces. When the Americans were in striking distance, Washington ordered General Charles Lee to attack the red-coats with part of the army. Lee, an English-born

Henry Clinton

131

soldier who had joined the American side, was supposed to attack at dawn on June 28, 1778. For some reason he waited until almost 8 A.M. to begin fighting the Battle of Monmouth.

Not only had Lee waited too long to start the battle, he did something strange once the fighting began. He suddenly ordered his men to retreat. When George Washington approached with the main army, he was enraged about this. General Henry Knox reported that Washington was so angry at Lee that he "swore that day till the leaves shook on the trees."

Washington sent the retreating troops back into battle along with his own main army. The Battle of Monmouth lasted all day and was fought in temperatures close to 100 degrees F. The intense heat, which caused many men on both sides to collapse from sunstroke, contributed to one of the war's most famous episodes.

In those days, women sometimes entered the battlefield to bring their men food and drink. Mary Ludwig Hays, who had been born near Trenton, New Jersey, joined her husband John at the Battle of Monmouth. When she saw that many American soldiers were fainting from the heat, she began bringing them pitchers of water from a nearby well. After hearing her husband call her

Molly Pitcher took her husband's place after he fell at the Battle of Monmouth.

"Molly" as a nickname, the soldiers began calling her "Molly Pitcher" because of the water she brought them.

Twenty-three-year-old Molly Pitcher did more than just provide the men with water at the Battle of Monmouth. When her husband collapsed—from either a gunshot wound or the heat—she took his place at his cannon and stayed there until the battle ended. She was one of only a handful of women who actually fought in the Revolutionary War.

Although the British had 400 dead and wounded compared with 250 for the Americans,

The arrest of General Charles Lee

the Battle of Monmouth was considered a draw because the Americans couldn't stop Clinton from marching his army across New Jersey to New York City. General Charles Lee and Mary Ludwig Hays met very different fates after the Battle of Monmouth. George Washington, who felt that Lee had turned traitor and tried to lose the battle, had him court-martialed for "misbehaving before the enemy." Lee was found guilty, suspended, and later dismissed from the army. Molly Pitcher, on the other hand, was thanked personally by George Washington for her bravery.

Many lesser-known Revolutionary War clashes took place in New Jersey besides the battles at Trenton, Princeton, and Monmouth. The Battle of Red Bank, which took place south of Camden, New Jersey, on October 22, 1777, and the Battle of Paulus Hook, which was fought in what is now downtown Jersey City on August 19, 1779, were two important American victories.

Before finally winning the Revolutionary War, the Continental Army had to survive another ordeal in New Jersey. George Washington decided to spend the winter of 1779–80 with his army at Morristown, New Jersey, as he had done three years earlier. Since parts of the army had spent the winter of 1778–79 near Somerville, New Jersey, this marked the third time in four years that the American troops had gone into winter quarters in New Jersey. The exception was the winter of 1777–78, which the army had spent at Valley Forge, Pennsylvania, before fighting the Battle of Monmouth.

Unfortunately, the winter of 1779–80 was one of the century's worst in New Jersey. It snowed about 30 times, with one blizzard piling four feet of snow on the ground. About 12,000 men spent that awful winter in huts, while George Washington and his wife, Martha, made the Ford Mansion in Morristown their headquarters. At times the soldiers went "five or six days together without bread" and "ate every kind of horse food but hay," George Washington reported.

Washington's army survived that dreadful winter at Morristown, and the Americans finally began to win the war in 1780 and 1781, especially in the South. In August 1781, Washington led his troops once more through New Jersey on the way south to fight a huge battle against the redcoats at Yorktown, Virginia. French soldiers and sailors helped the Americans win the Battle of Yorktown in October 1781. This crucial American victory marked the end of major Revolutionary War fighting, though the war didn't officially end until the fall of 1783 when the United States and Britain signed a peace treaty.

New Jersey and the other twelve states had done what had seemed almost impossible. They had beaten the world's most powerful nation, and in doing so they had transformed the thirteen colonies into the United States of America.

MOLLY PITCHER (1754–1832)

Mary Ludwig was born on October 13, 1754, into a German-American family that lived near Trenton, New Jersey. For about the first 14 years of her life, Mary lived on her family's dairy farm. The Ludwigs were not rich, and so in 1769 Mary went to work as a servant for a family that lived in Carlisle, Pennsylvania, across the Delaware River and about 125 miles west of Trenton.

Molly Pitcher

In July 1769, when she was not quite 15, Mary Ludwig married a barber named John Hays in Carlisle. After the Revolutionary War broke out six years later, John became a gunner in the Continental Army. Mary then moved back to her parent's home near Trenton so that she could be near her husband. She followed him to the Battle of Monmouth. On that scorching hot Sunday in June 1778, Mary earned a place in American folklore by bringing the men water and firing her husband's cannon after he collapsed. Not only did George Washington thank Molly Pitcher and make her a sergeant, but John recovered. Molly Pitcher reportedly served in the Continental Army for another few years, and may have taken part in other battles.

After the war, Molly and John returned to Carlisle, Pennsylvania. They raised a son, who was also named John. Unfortunately, Mary's husband died in 1789. She then married a man who reportedly abused her and lived on the money she earned by cooking, scrubbing, caring for children, and running a little store in Carlisle. In 1822, when Molly Pitcher was nearly 70 years old, she was granted a pension of $40 a year by the Pennsylvania legislature in recognition of her bravery at the Battle of Monmouth 44 years earlier. Molly Pitcher died at the age 77 in Carlisle, Pennsylvania.

George Washington (center) presided over the Constitutional Convention.

Chapter IX

The Third State

The business [creating the United States Constitution] is difficult and unavoidably takes up much time, but I think we shall eventually agree upon and adopt a system that will give strength and harmony to the Union and render us a great and happy people. This is the wish of every good, and the interest of every wise man.

From a letter William Paterson, a New Jersey delegate to the Constitutional Convention, wrote to his wife in July 1787

Those people who had expected Britain to squash the American Revolution had been proved wrong, but for most of the 1780s it appeared that the United States as a nation would collapse on its own. Although the individual states were strong, the national government was a disaster, largely because it had little power.

Most Americans favored a weak central government—at least until the situation got *very* bad in the late 1780s. For one thing, people feared that a strong national government would tax them more than the British had taxed them. For another, in those days when few people went far from home, nearly everyone cared more about their own state than they did about the nation as a whole. Even the way people wrote the country's name showed the emphasis on the states. People often wrote "united States" rather than "United States," because they didn't think of the two words as referring to one country.

The nation was loosely held together under a paper called the Articles of Confederation, which had gone into effect in 1781. The Articles were more noteworthy for what they *didn't* say than what they *did* say. Under the Articles, the country had no president and no national courts, money, or taxes. When the Continental Congress (the American government) needed money, it had to beg the states for it. Typically, the states gave Congress less than a tenth of the money it requested in a year. As a result, the U.S. government couldn't always pay its bills. In addition, the national government broke some of its promises to other nations, thereby losing much of the world's respect. There was even danger that the United States would be conquered by England or another country.

To top things off, the United States lacked a permanent national capital. Much of the time between 1776 and 1800, when Washington, D.C., finally became the permanent capital, few Americans could have even named their country's capital! The reason for this was that the capital was changed 10 different times in that quarter century. During the 1780s, two New Jersey cities briefly served as the national capital. Princeton was the U.S. capital from June 30 to November 4, 1783. Trenton served as the seat of government from November 1 to December 24, 1784.

The way Princeton became the U.S. capital illustrates the pitiful state of the national government. In June 1783, about 100 soldiers who were owed back pay by the U.S. government marched on Philadelphia, which was then the nation's capital. On June 21, 1783, the soldiers surrounded the Capitol building. They yelled that they wanted their money, and some of them broke windows and poked their guns through the holes. Since Congress lacked the money to pay the men, the national lawmakers ran away like characters in an old movie comedy! They crossed the Delaware River to Princeton, New Jersey, which nine days later became the U.S. capital.

It took even more dramatic events to convince most Americans that a stronger, better-organized national government was needed. One of those events involved the ratification (approval) of the treaty ending the Revolutionary War. This treaty, which was favorable to the United States, was supposed to be ratified by Congress and returned to Paris, France, by March 3, 1784. The problem was, at least nine of the thirteen states had to approve the treaty. In those days, some states didn't always bother to send representatives to Congress. By the end of 1783, only seven states were sufficiently represented in Congress, which was then meeting in Annapolis, Maryland. It wasn't until February 14, 1784, that nine states were properly represented. Congress approved the treaty that day, but since it took a few weeks to ship things to Europe, the signed treaty reached Paris a month past the deadline. Fortunately, England didn't use this as an excuse to back out of the treaty ending the war.

Shays' Rebellion also demonstrated the weakness of the national government. Led by Daniel Shays, this was a revolt by western Massachusetts farmers that occurred between September 1786 and February 1787. The farmers were protesting high Massachusetts taxes and unjust laws that jailed debtors. The U.S. Army, consisting of only about 700 men, couldn't end Shays' Rebellion, so the Massachusetts militia had to do the job.

By 1787 most Americans wanted a stronger national government, and in spring of that year a big convention opened in Philadelphia to create it. At first the delegates planned only to revise the Articles of Confederation, but instead they made a whole new set of national laws called the Constitution of the United States.

Every state but Rhode Island sent delegates to the Constitutional Convention. New Jersey sent five men—William Livingston, William Paterson, David Brearley, William Churchill Houston, and Jonathan Dayton. Livingston was currently New Jersey's governor. Paterson would become New Jersey's state governor in 1790, and would have the city of Paterson, New Jersey, named for him. Brearley was chief justice of the New Jersey Supreme Court. Houston had been a mathematics professor at Princeton College. Just 26 years old when the Constitutional Convention opened, Dayton (for whom the city of Dayton, Ohio, was later named) was the youngest man at this important meeting.

Various plans of government were presented at the Constitutional Convention. Virginia offered the Virginia Plan, which would have made the states with large populations much stronger than those with smaller populations in the national

William Paterson

Jonathan Dayton

legislature. New Jersey countered with the New Jersey Plan. Presented by William Paterson, the New Jersey Plan would have made each state equally powerful in the national legislature, regardless of population. In the end this conflict was settled by the Connecticut Compromise, which provided the type of national legislature we have today. States with large populations have more members in the House of Representatives than less-populous states. However, each state has two U.S. senators, regardless of its size.

Upon its completion in the early fall of 1787, the Constitution was signed by representatives of all the states but Rhode Island. William Churchill Houston didn't sign the Constitution because illness had forced him to leave the convention early. But New Jersey's four other delegates—William Livingston, William Paterson, David Brearley, and Jonathan Dayton—signed it.

The delegates had decided that each of the former thirteen colonies would become a state under the new United States Constitution when they approved the document. They had also decided that the Constitution would take effect after nine states had ratified it.

Three neighbors along the Delaware River were the first to ratify the Constitution. Delaware

The senators and representatives beforementioned, and the members of the several state legiſ-latures, and all executive and judicial officers, both of the United States and of the several States, ſhall be bound by oath or affirmation, to ſupport this conſtitution; but no religious teſt ſhall ever be required as a qualification to any office or public truſt under the United States.

VII.

The ratification of the conventions of nine States, ſhall be sufficient for the eſtabliſhment of this conſtitution between the States ſo ratifying the ſame:

Done in Convention, by the unanimous conſent of the

States preſent, the ſeventeenth day of September, in the year of our Lord one thouſand ſeven hundred and eighty-ſeven, and of the Independence of the United States of America the twelfth. In witneſs whereof we have hereunto ſubſcribed our Names.

GEORGE WASHINGTON, Preſident,

And Deputy from VIRGINIA.

NEW-HAMPSHIRE.	John Langdon, Nicholas Gilman.		George Read, Gunning Bedford, Junior,
MASSACHUSETTS.	Nathaniel Gorham, Rufus King.	DELAWARE.	John Dickinſon, Richard Baſſett, Jacob Broom.
CONNECTICUT	William Samuel Johnſon, Roger Sherman.		James M·Henry,
NEW-YORK.	Alexander Hamilton.	MARYLAND.	Daniel of St. Tho Jenifer, Daniel Carrol.
NEW-JERSEY.	William Livingſton, David Brearley, William Paterſon, Jonathan Dayton.	VIRGINIA.	John Blair, James Madiſon, Junior.
		NORTH-CAROLINA	William Blount, Richard Dobbs Spaight, Hugh Williamſon.
PENNSYLVANIA.	Benjamin Franklin, Thomas M·fflin, Robert Morris, George Clymer, Thomas Fitzſimons, Jared Ingerſoll, James Wilſon, Gouverneur Morris.	SOUTH-CAROLINA.	John Rutledge, Charles Cotesworth Pinckney Charles Pinckney. Pierce Butler.
		GEORGIA.	William Few, Abraham Baldwin.

Atteſt, William Jackſon, SECRETARY.

IN CONVENTION, Monday September 17th, 1787.
PRESENT

The States of New-Hampſhire, Maſſachuſetts, Connecticut, Mr. *Hamilton* from New-York, New-Jerſey, Pennſylvania, Delaware, Maryland, Virginia, North-Carolina, South-Carolina and Georgia:

RESOLVED,

THAT the preceding Conſtitution be laid before the United States in Congreſs aſſembled, and that it is the opinion of this Convention, that it ſhould afterwards be ſubmitted to a Convention of Delegates, choſen in each State by the People thereof, under the recommendation of its Legiſlature, for their aſſent and ratification; and that each Convention aſſenting to, and ratifying the ſame, ſhould give Notice thereof to the United States in Congreſs aſſembled.

Reſolved, That it is the opinion of this Convention, that as ſoon as the Conventions of nine States ſhall have ratified this Conſtitution, the United States in Congreſs aſſembled ſhould fix a day on which Electors ſhould be appointed by the States which ſhall have ratified the ſame, and a day on which the Electors ſhould aſſemble to vote for the Preſident, and the time and place for commencing proceedings under this Conſtitution. That after ſuch publication the Electors ſhould be appointed, and the Senators and Repreſentatives elected: That the Electors ſhould meet on the day fixed for the Election of the Preſident, and ſhould tranſmit their votes certified, ſigned, ſealed and directed, as the Conſtitution requires, to the Secretary of the United States in Congreſs aſſembled, that the Senators and Repreſentatives ſhould convene at the time and place aſſigned; that the Senators ſhould appoint a Preſident of the Senate, for the ſole purpoſe of receiving, opening and counting the votes for Preſident; and, that after he ſhall be choſen, the Congreſs, together with the Preſident, ſhould, without delay, proceed to execute this Conſtitution.

By the unanimous Order of the Convention,

GEORGE WASHINGTON, Preſident.

William Jackſon, Secretary

The last page of the U.S. Constitution, with the names of the delegates who signed the document earned the nickname the *First State* by approving the Constitution on December 7, 1787, before any other state. Pennsylvania became the second state just five days later on December 12, 1787. Just six days after that, on December 18, 1787, delegates to a New Jersey convention approved the Constitution at the Blazing Star Tavern in Trenton.

People in Trenton (which became the state capital in 1790) and other towns cheered when they heard that New Jersey had approved the Constitution. For with that vote, New Jersey—which had been the scene of the battles of Trenton, Princeton, and Monmouth, the home of the Lenni-Lenape Indians, Patience Lovell Wright, and Reverend John Witherspoon, and the site of two temporary U.S. capitals—became the third state. The United States Constitution went into effect in June 1788 when the ninth state, New Hampshire, ratified it, and in May 1790 stubborn little Rhode Island became the last of the original thirteen colonies to approve the Constitution.

WILLIAM LIVINGSTON (1723-1790)

William Livingston was born into a prominent family in Albany, New York. He was raised mainly by his grandmother in Albany, but when he was 14 he went to live for a year with an English missionary to New York's Mohawk Indians. William's family thought that living out in the wilderness for a time would help him if he later entered the fur business or bought land on the frontier.

After returning home, William enrolled in Connecticut's Yale College, graduating in 1741. He then studied law with James Alexander, a New York City lawyer who a few years earlier had fought for freedom of the press in a famous trial of a newspaper publisher. William was still studying law in 1745 when he married Susanna French, whose father was a rich New Jersey landowner. William and Susanna eventually had thirteen children.

William Livingston

Soon after he was licensed in 1748, William Livingston became known as one of the best lawyers in New York and New Jersey. He fought for some of the basic liberties that Americans prize today. For example, he fought for the separation of church and government during the early 1750s, when King's College (now Columbia University) was being founded in New York City. Some people wanted the Church of England to dominate the college, but Livingston thought it shouldn't be controlled by any one church and should admit people of various faiths. In 1758, he was elected to the New York legislature, where he opposed interference by the English Parliament in colonial affairs.

Starting in about 1760, Livingston bought land near Elizabeth, New Jersey. After his political party in New York began losing power, he moved to New Jersey in the early 1770s and built a mansion called "Liberty Hall" near Elizabeth. Although Livingston still worked on a legal case now and then, he lived in semi-retirement for several years. He spent his time growing vegetables and fruit trees and helping to raise his large family.

The Revolutionary War drew him back into public affairs. He was elected to represent New Jersey in both the First and Second Continental Congresses, and would have signed the Declaration of Independence (as his older brother, Philip, did for New York) if he hadn't had to take command of the New Jersey militia in June 1776. William Livingston wasn't a soldier and he even joked that the British would rather hang him for the papers he had written against them than for his military ability. He was happy when he was relieved of his military command and was elected New Jersey's first state governor in late August 1776. He was re-elected governor again and again for the rest of his life.

Since New Jersey had many Loyalists and was occupied by British troops, Governor Livingston's job was very dangerous and difficult. The British offered a huge reward for his capture, resulting in many attempts to kidnap or kill him. For about six years, just to survive, he never slept more than two consecutive nights under the same roof. Through all these hardships, Livingston did all he could to keep New Jersey running and to supply the Continental Army with soldiers from his state.

After the Revolutionary War ended, William Livingston showed that he really believed that "all men are created equal," as is stated in the Declaration of Independence. He joined an organization that was dedicated to freeing slaves, and freed the only two slaves that he owned. Because they were considered valuable property, slaves were rarely freed in colonial times.

In 1787, William Livingston was appointed one of New Jersey's delegates to the Constitutional Convention in Philadelphia. He signed the Constitution and was largely responsible for New Jersey's quick approval of the great paper. New Jersey's first state governor died in Elizabeth, New Jersey, less than three years later at the age of 66.

The signers of the Declaration of Independence

IN CONGRESS, JULY 4, 1776

The unanimous Declaration of the thirteen united States of America,

The Declaration of Independence

Colonial America Time Line

Before the arrival of Europeans, many millions of Indians belonging to dozens of tribes lived in North America (and also in Central and South America)

About A.D. 982—Eric the Red, born in Norway, reaches Greenland during one of the first European voyages to North America

About 985—Eric the Red brings settlers from Iceland to Greenland

About 1000—Leif Ericson (Eric the Red's son) leads what is thought to be the first European expedition to mainland North America; Leif probably lands in Canada

1492—Christopher Columbus, sailing for Spain, reaches America

1497—John Cabot reaches Canada in the first English voyage to North America

1513—Ponce de León of Spain explores Florida

1519-1521—Hernando Cortés of Spain conquers Mexico

1565—St. Augustine, Florida, the first permanent European town in what is now the United States, is founded by the Spanish

1607—Jamestown, Virginia, is founded, the first permanent English town in the present-day United States

1608—Frenchman Samuel de Champlain founds the village of Quebec, Canada

1609—Henry Hudson explores the eastern coast of present-day United States for The Netherlands; the Dutch then claim parts of New York, New Jersey, Delaware, and Connecticut and name the area New Netherland

1619—Virginia's House of Burgesses, America's first representative lawmaking body, is founded

1619—The first shipment of black slaves arrives in Jamestown

1620—English Pilgrims found Massachusetts' first permanent town at Plymouth

1621—Massachusetts Pilgrims and Indians hold the famous first Thanksgiving feast in colonial America

1622—Indians kill 347 settlers in Virginia

1623—Colonization of New Hampshire is begun by the English

1624—Colonization of present-day New York State is begun by the Dutch at Fort Orange (Albany)

1625—The Dutch start building New Amsterdam (now New York City)

1630—The town of Boston, Massachusetts, is founded by the English Puritans

1633—Colonization of Connecticut is begun by the English

1634—Colonization of Maryland is begun by the English

1635—Boston Latin School, the colonies' first public school, is founded

1636—Harvard, the colonies' first college, is founded in Massachusetts

1636—Rhode Island colonization begins when Englishman Roger Williams founds Providence

1638—The colonies' first library is established at Harvard

1638—Delaware colonization begins when Swedish people build Fort Christina at present-day Wilmington

1640—Stephen Daye of Cambridge, Massachusetts, prints *The Bay Psalm Book*, the first English-language book published in what is now the United States

1643—Swedish settlers begin colonizing Pennsylvania

1647—Massachusetts forms the first public school system in the colonies

1650—North Carolina is colonized by Virginia settlers in about this year

1650—Population of colonial United States is about 50,000

1660—New Jersey colonization is begun by the Dutch at present-day Jersey City

1670—South Carolina colonization is begun by the English near Charleston

1673—Jacques Marquette and Louis Jolliet explore the upper Mississippi River for France

1675-76—New England colonists beat Indians in King Philip's War

1682—Philadelphia, Pennsylvania, is settled

1682—La Salle explores Mississippi River all the way to its mouth in Louisiana and claims the whole Mississippi Valley for France

1693—College of William and Mary is founded in Williamsburg, Virginia

1700—Colonial population is about 250,000

1704—*The Boston News-Letter*, the first successful newspaper in the colonies, is founded

1706—Benjamin Franklin is born in Boston

1732—George Washington, future first president of the United States, is born in Virginia

1733—English begin colonizing Georgia, their thirteenth colony in what is now the United States

1735—John Adams, future second president, is born in Massachusetts

1743—Thomas Jefferson, future third president, is born in Virginia

1750—Colonial population is about 1,200,000

1754—France and England begin fighting the French and Indian War over North American lands

1763—England, victorious in the war, gains Canada and most other French lands east of the Mississippi River

1764—British pass Sugar Act to gain tax money from the colonists

1765—British pass the Stamp Act, which the colonists despise; colonists then hold the Stamp Act Congress in New York City

1766—British repeal the Stamp Act

1770—British soldiers kill five Americans in the "Boston Massacre"

1773—Colonists dump British tea into Boston Harbor at the "Boston Tea Party"

1774—British close up port of Boston to punish the city for the tea party

1774—Delegates from all the colonies but Georgia meet in Philadelphia at the First Continental Congress

1775—**April 19:** Revolutionary war begins at Lexington and Concord, Massachusetts

       May 10: Second Continental Congress convenes in Philadelphia

       June 17: Colonists inflict heavy losses on British but lose Battle of Bunker Hill near Boston

       July 3: George Washington takes command of Continental Army

1776—**March 17:** Washington's troops force the British out of Boston in the first major American win of the war

       May 4: Rhode Island is first colony to declare itself independent of Britain

July 4: Declaration of Independence is adopted

December 26: Washington's forces win Battle of Trenton (New Jersey)

1777—January 3: Americans win at Princeton, New Jersey

August 16: Americans win Battle of Bennington at New York-Vermont border

September 11: British win Battle of Brandywine Creek near Philadelphia

September 26: British capture Philadelphia

October 4: British win Battle of Germantown near Philadelphia

October 17: About 5,000 British troops surrender at Battle of Saratoga in New York

December 19: American army goes into winter quarters at Valley Forge, Pennsylvania, where more than 3,000 of them die by spring

1778—February 6: France joins the American side

July 4: American George Rogers Clark captures Kaskaskia, Illinois, from the British

1779—February 23-25: George Rogers Clark captures Vincennes in Indiana

September 23: American John Paul Jones captures British ship *Serapis*

1780—May 12: British take Charleston, South Carolina

August 16: British badly defeat Americans at Camden, South Carolina

October 7: Americans defeat British at Kings Mountain, South Carolina

1781—January 17: Americans win battle at Cowpens, South Carolina

March 1: Articles of Confederation go into effect as laws of the United States

March 15: British suffer heavy losses at Battle of Guilford Courthouse in North Carolina; British then give up most of North Carolina

October 19: British army under Charles Cornwallis surrenders at Yorktown, Virginia, as major Revolutionary War fighting ends

1783—September 3: United States officially wins Revolution as the United States and Great Britain sign Treaty of Paris

November 25: Last British troops leave New York City

1787—On December 7, Delaware becomes the first state by approving the U.S. Constitution

1788—On June 21, New Hampshire becomes the ninth state when it approves the U.S. Constitution; with nine states having approved it, the Constitution goes into effect as the law of the United States

1789—On April 30, George Washington is inaugurated as first president of the United States

1790—On May 29, Rhode Island becomes the last of the original thirteen colonies to become a state

1791—U.S. Bill of Rights goes into effect on December 15

INDEX- *Page numbers in boldface type indicate illustrations.*

About the Author

Dennis Brindell Fradin is the author of more than 100 published children's books. His works for Childrens Press include the Young People's Stories of Our States series, the Disaster! series, and the Thirteen Colonies series. His other books are *Remarkable Children* (Little, Brown), which is about twenty children who made history, and a science-fiction novel entitled *How I Saved the World* (Dillon). Dennis is married to Judith Bloom Fradin, a high-school English teacher. They have two sons named Tony and Mike and a daughter named Diana Judith. Dennis was graduated from Northwestern University in 1967 with a B.A. in creative writing, and has lived in Evanston, Illinois, since that year.

Photo Credits